Housing (

José Ospina

Hilary Shipman
London

First published 1987 by
Hilary Shipman Limited
19 Framfield Road
Highbury
London N5 1UU

British Library Cataloguing in Publication Data
Ospina, José
    Housing Ourselves.
    1. Housing, Cooperative—Great Britain—
        History—20th century
    2. Housing, Cooperative—Latin America—
        History—20th century
    I. Title
    334'.1'0941   HD7287.72.G7

ISBN 0-948096-08-X
ISBN 0-948096-09-8 Pbk

Cover design by David Bennett
Data conversion by ImagePlus
Typeset in Oxford by Infotype Limited
Printed and bound by Biddles Limited
Guildford & King's Lynn

Contents

Acknowledgements

This book could not have taken shape without the patient support of my wife Alison, the help and encouragement of the Institute of Advanced Architectural Studies in York, and, more recently, of my publishers. I am also grateful to those who have contributed information: Janet Shearer and Michael Lyneton for Bristol; Charlotte Ellis and Colin Ward for Lewisham; Nick Wates, Anne Grosskurth and David Innes Wilkin for Liverpool; Caroline Murdoch for Glasgow; Diana Rodriguez, Eliecer Ortega and Beatriz de Ospina for Colombia; and the *Architects' Journal* for permission to quote material. Most of all, I would like to thank those colleagues whom I have had the good luck to work with and learn from during the last 14 years. I hope this book does justice to their often unacknowledged efforts.

The author

José Ospina was born in Bogota in Colombia. He came to England in 1972, and in 1973, while a postgraduate film student at Bristol University, he helped start the Self-Help Community Housing Association, subsequently working there as the co-ordinator. Since then, he has worked in community housing in Britain and – for two years – in Colombia. In 1985 he gained an MA from the Institute of Advanced Architectural Studies at the University of York for his researches into community housing. He is now development worker for CHISEL Ltd (Co-operative Housing in South-East London). He is married and has two children.

Preface

My intention in initiating the research that led to the writing of this book was to look at many examples, throughout the world, of housing projects where participation had been practised, to look at the various methods that had been applied in different circumstances, and to try to draw up a sort of 'manual' detailing the steps that could be followed in the setting up of such projects. This idea was abandoned at an early stage because I did not want to suggest that a mechanical application of methods or procedures would necessarily lead to succesful projects. Rather, it is a question of adopting the appropriate methods and taking the appropriate steps for a given context, in pursuit of the fundamental objective of popular control that will make for success. Even then, circumstances might defeat these initiatives.

As an alternative form of presentation, I opted for summarised descriptions of selected projects that fulfilled the desired characteristics, together with a brief overview of the main economic, political and historical circumstances that made these developments possible. This is not intended to suggest that these background factors in themselves determine the existence or success of popular participation, merely that the harmony of 'internal' and 'external' factors must be taken into account in developing such projects.

Finally, I have attempted to draw some general conclusions, both from each case history and from all the material, which attempt to interpret these experiences and sketch a general model of participatory housing.

In order to do justice to the projects described in this book and their contexts, I have only attempted to recount projects in which I have been directly involved, or whose details I am sufficiently familiar with to describe in detail.

I would emphasise that the results are the empirical conclusions of a housing worker, rather than the scientific research of an academic. I cannot pretend it contains all the information or answers all the questions – but at least it provides a broad introduction to someone who wants to look into the subject. The best way to find out more is to visit the projects, and the many others like them, personally.

José Ospina

1 | Popular participation in housing

In December 1982, the United Nations General Assembly unanimously adopted a resolution proclaiming 1987 as International Year of Shelter for the Homeless. One of the main objectives of the Year would be:

> Developing and demonstrating new approaches and methods to assist directly and augment the present efforts of the homeless, poor and disadvantaged to secure their own shelter. . .

The Assembly merely echoed a principle already accepted by many Third World governments and international development agencies. A report to the 1976 UN Conference on Uncontrolled Urban Settlements stated:

> Of all the resources now being devoted to improvement of conditions in slums and squatter settlements, those of people themselves are by far the most significant.

The new popularity of this approach was primarily due to the work of one man, John Turner. A Londoner and graduate of the Architectural Association, Turner worked in Peru from 1957 to 1965, mainly on the promotion and design of community action and self-help programmes in villages and urban squatter settlements. His experiences were consolidated in the United States, where he was employed by the Department of Housing and Urban Development. The result was the book *Freedom to Build*, in which he first stated the basic principles of the 'self-help' approach to low-income housing:

> When dwellers control the major decisions and are free to make their own contribution to the design, construction or

management of their housing, both the process and the environment produced stimulate individual and social well-being. When people have no control over, nor responsibility for, key decisions in the housing process, on the other hand, dwelling environments may instead become a barrier to personal fulfilment and a burden on the economy.

Developing these principles (some say misinterpreting them), many national and international agencies turned away from the provision of finished 'mass housing' schemes, to the provision of 'site and services' – essentially a serviced plot of land where the poor could build for themselves. These schemes sometimes aroused controversy: some thought they allowed governments to evade their responsibility to provide housing directly; others felt that they diverted popular struggles into relatively harmless reforms.

In spite of the criticisms, the popularity of the schemes has demonstrated that self-help is still the only reliable, universal source of housing for the poor. And there is an arsenal of evidence to support this view. Hundreds of studies are available on the achievements and shortcomings of such schemes all over the world, and written from every conceivable point of view from glowing to damning, from impressionistic to statistical – demonstrating, if nothing else, the currency and universality of the movement.

One example is Paul Harrison's book *Third World Tomorrow*. Harrison gives several examples of self-help in housing, based on his own research. One is the Leoncio Prado township near Lima, where thousands of migrant families have built their own town. Another is the Study Action Group of Ahmedabad in India, that has 'enabled' 2,000 families to build homes and develop their communities. Yet another is the Tondo squatters' federation in Manila, which forced the hard-line Marcos government to consult them on the city's Urban Plan. More accounts may be found in Geoffrey Payne's *Low Income Housing in the Developing Countries*, including Fundasal, the Salvadorean non-profit foundation that helps 1,400 people a year build their own homes, and the 'Freedom to Build' group, again in Manila, which has helped 4,000 families house themselves. Other cases have been documented in Chile, Nicaragua, Uruguay, Zambia, Turkey, Portugal and Egypt. The list is long.

In the face of these examples, a view of participation in housing in Britain would be incomplete without reference to this international dimension. The parallels are evident and enlightening, and serve to underline the lessons of each experience. This is something I am personally very conscious of as a result of working in two countries: Britain and Colombia.

As a student in Bristol, in 1973, I co-founded the city's Student Community Housing Association, later to be the Self-Help Community Housing Association, and worked with the organisation until 1982. Returning to Colombia, I had the opportunity to work for the Simon Bolivar Association of Popular Housing and, later, the government's Territorial Housing Institute, Colombia's main provider of subsidised housing. Finally, I helped start up Fedevivienda, the country's first federation of self-help housing groups, before returning to Britain to write a research thesis, based on my experiences, at the University of York.

In an attempt to convey this international dimension, this book includes three chapters on Colombia to give readers some idea of how parallel developments in fact are. While not wanting to underplay the obvious contrasts in background and present conditions, it is still evident that similar forces are at work in both countries. My view is that Third World countries are not living in the past of the developed nations, but represent the poor neighbourhoods of the world, intrinsically linked with the wealthier ones.

International Year of Shelter for the Homeless finds the movement in both countries at a critical stage of development. Community housing initiatives are now on the agenda in both countries. In Colombia they have been adopted within the housing programme of the present government. In Britain they have become the focus of political debate and media attention. There is, however, much misunderstanding as to what these initiatives really mean and how they can go forward. The situation is further confused by apparent moves by powerful interest groups to 'kidnap' the movement for the benefit of their particular aims.

Leading figures in the architectural establishment, for instance, have recently attempted to define the trend for user-control of housing as 'community architecture', picking out that particular aspect of its activities. I would not deny that 'enabling' architectural services are important if people are to control their own housing, but that is not the primary motive of the movement. There are many other ingredients that go into the equation, which need study and support.

There is, for instance, a need to create the financial and legal framework where communities can really take control, to remove the bureaucratic obstacles to self-management and to adequately train users to understand all aspects of the housing process. This will certainly not be achieved by aggrandising the role of one set of professionals while disregarding that of the other necessary participants, particularly the community itself. Community architecture must be seen in its real perspective – as an essential but not central part in the model.

Similarly, we have seen recent attempts by various political parties to manipulate co-ops for their own benefit. Conservative and Alliance parties, for example, have used the Liverpool co-ops as a battering ram against the Labour council, giving them a level of official support that was certainly not typical of the rest of the country as a whole. In contrast, the response of the DoE and the Scottish Office to the community ownership proposal by Glasgow council has been to obstruct and delay these schemes by inserting the Housing Corporation into the equation in an apparent attempt to gain more central control of the initiatives.

And in England, legislation, for example the Local Government Act 1986, threatens to torpedo a whole host of schemes involving local authority support of short-life and co-operative housing schemes, and through the Housing and Planning Act 1986 aims to create tenant co-operatives in council estates, irrespective of the wishes of the authority concerned.

The irony of foisting co-ops on councils that don't want them, while blocking the schemes put forward by the councils that do, must not be lost on us. But such opportunism is bound to undermine and demoralise those who are promoting such initiatives seriously.

It is clear that until the community housing movement defines its own identity and objectives, it will be prone to manipulation from different quarters in the attempt to use it as a pawn in their particular games. This is as true for Colombia as for Britain. It would appear that the future of the community housing initiatives in Britain and Colombia, and probably everywhere else, is dependent on the extent to which they can come together as a cohesive national and international movement, conscious of their role and possibilities, and free of manipulative professional and political influences.

A final note is provided by Gregory Andrusz, a researcher at the Middlesex Polytechnic. It appears that housing co-operatives were popular in the Soviet Union, even after the October Revolution, only abolished after the 'Stalin Constitution' of 1936. In the 1960s, with a move away from orthodoxy, they resurfaced, gaining credibility as an alternative to the bureaucratic housing practices of the local 'soviets' (local authorities). Today, they have been singled out for attention. In February 1986, Mikhail Gorbachev gave a speech to the 27th Party Congress 'signalling the necessity to . . . expand and extend the activities of co-operatives of all kinds and to grant greater powers to local soviets to . . . decentralise and democratise the decision-making process.'

It would appear, then, that 'glasnost' can also mean 'housing ourselves'. . .

2 | Foundations

The Age of Professions will be remembered as the time when politics withered, when voters, guided by professors, entrusted to technocrats the power to legislate needs, renounced the authority to decide who needs what, and suffered monopolistic oligarchies to determine the means by which these needs shall be met. (*Disabling Professions*, Ivan Illich)

The background to the present book is my experience of over 14 years' work with self-help housing groups and government housing bodies in Colombia and England. As a result of this varied experience, I have come into contact with the different housing models, and formed three basic, but by no means original, opinions about them:

1. *Profit-orientated use of resources by the private sector fails to meet the housing need of low-income people.*

This is as evident today as it has been in the past. The private housing sector, without any interference from the state, created the appalling slum conditions recorded in Victorian England. Today, with the relaxation of state intervention in low-income housing, we see similar conditions emerging in the bed-and-breakfast accommodation provided for homeless families. In Colombia the private rented sector is still a primary source of housing for persons on low incomes, and conditions are probably worse than they were in Victorian England. The problem is not that the private sector does not have the resources, financial and technical, to provide adequate housing for these people but that it does not have the motivation, given the modest returns.

2. *State control of public resources intended to provide housing for low-income people usually fails to achieve this aim adequately.*

Some would argue that this is merely the result of not enough resources being available, or of official standards not being high

6

enough. The amount of money available will, of course, limit the technical standards and the number of housing units that are provided. But resources will not on their own guarantee that the housing will be adequate or appropriate for the people being housed. Council tenants in a high-rise estate are more likely to be dissatisfied with their housing, although it might have been more expensive and designed to higher standards, than co-op members who have helped design their own homes. Neither will having enough resources guarantee that public housing will be sensitively and efficiently managed or effectively maintained.

There is also evidence, in both Colombia and England, that public housing rarely goes to those in most need, who continue to be denied access to subsidised housing by virtue of arbitrary criteria.
3. *Popular control of even limited resources leads to the production of more appropriate low-income housing.*
I mean by 'popular control' direct control by the users, by the people being housed. Perhaps the best example of this is the occurrence of the 'illegal' settlements of Colombia and other Third World countries, built primarily by the residents themselves, using their own resources. Although conditions in these settlements are far from ideal, usually lacking access to basic services and built without the benefit of planning, they do at least succeed in housing the country's low-income population, where government housing schemes fail. What could these people have achieved if, as well as their own resources, they had access to technical and financial support from the state?

In Britain, with its tradition of state responsibility for low-income housing, examples of popular control of housing resources are unusual. But those recorded, like the licensed squatting movement of the 1970s, show that homeless people in Britain can also house themselves reasonably well even with limited resources (empty houses, modest rental income), as long as those resources are under their control.

Technical or financial problems, or problems of control

The traditional critique of 'the housing question' is to attribute the failure of the various policies to financial or technical causes. Both explanations fail to get to the real cause of the problem. The financial argument holds that if enough (usually public) money is made available, good housing will be provided for all. It does not explain how inadequate housing (notorious examples of municipal housing, for instance) has been produced in spite of funding being available, and why increased funding should not simply lead to more of the same.

The technical argument runs parallel to this, arguing that if greater technology were introduced, better housing would be achieved. This again is not borne out by the response of residents in systems-built estates, by comparison with the evident satisfaction of residents in more 'primitive' homes.

An inversion of this argument is also sometimes found. If less public money is made available for housing, then its quality will improve, or if more primitive technologies are used more appropriate housing will be produced. The logic of this is faulty, and certainly not borne out in practice. Reduced cost limits simply mean a reduction in standards, and simpler building technologies can also be misapplied and lead to new technical problems (e.g. problems with mass production of timber-frame houses).

A less superficial approach is to define what we mean by 'good' and 'bad' housing. Good for whom; bad for whom? Do we mean housing as a vehicle for the architect's personal expression, or housing that is appropriate for the users and satisfies them? Do we mean housing that provides a testing ground for the ultra-modern technologies of industry, or housing that is at a scale which residents can really handle? Do we mean housing that provides a solid asset for a financial institution, or housing which people can really afford? Do we mean housing programmes that satisfy the political objectives of the state, or housing tailored to people's real needs?

If our starting point is that 'good' and 'bad' housing can only be defined by *the users themselves* having the information and the power to make this decision, then it will follow that really good housing will only be achieved by placing available housing resources, and the process of creating housing, under user-control, so that they can make their own choices.

Housing from the top down

The profit-orientated, commercial housing process is usually initiated by investment capital being made available from private sources to design and build houses which later become consumer goods. A clear path in decision-making can then be traced downward from the financier, who is after a good return, to the developer, who wants a scheme he can sell, to the architect, who 'knows' what is pleasing and cost-effective, to the builder, who can work to the specifications for the agreed costs, and finally to the consumer, or user, who pays for the operation, plus a little more which allows the financier to start the process again.

State housing is supposed to be on the other side of the political fence, but in this sense is it that different? Government planners produce housing targets based on a 'scientific study of need', often tailored to political objectives. The Treasury allocates a budget and the architects at the appropriate government department specify 'housing units' that are supposed to fit neatly into predetermined 'cost-limits'. If the budget is reduced, cost-limits and standards are reduced. Builders, very often private, are then contracted to work to these specifications, cutting corners wherever viable to keep within cost-limits and to increase profit margins. At the end of the line are the users, selected after the state has 'quantified' their need on the basis of particular criteria (or some less 'objective' method of selection). These 'beneficiaries', like their commercial counterparts, will eventually, albeit collectively, pay for the whole process, in rent, taxes, or simply the exploitation of their labour. A little more will also be provided to enable the state to repeat the operation.

These are simplistic models, but they serve to illustrate that both traditional forms are essentially housing *from the top down*, where the last people to be given a say in the process are the users, although they are ultimately paying for it. I am not suggesting that in either case the interests of any particular group determine the product, but that there is a pyramidal hierarchy of interests, where those of the user are far down the list. Although it could be argued that in both instances the user has a measure of control, through 'the market' or Parliament or the Party, these channels of influence are too indirect to be effective. In practice, the interests and preferences of financiers, developers, civil servants, professionals and politicians are paramount, which is why, so far, they have shaped the provision of low-income housing in the models described.

The only exceptions to this norm will occur when people's income is so low that they are obliged to make their own provision, or when the principle of user-control is accepted and concrete methods are brought in to allow it to function.

Popular control and community organisation

In the 'illegal' settlements of the Third World, people generate their own resources and use them directly in housing themselves. The housing they produce is usually a very appropriate use of those resources, being based on an intimate knowledge of real needs and possibilities. Only the lack of organisation, technical knowledge and capital limit their outcome. But within those limitations there is a high level of common sense and traditional wisdom, as well as community support.

More effective forms of popular control, with the benefit of financial and professional resources, can be gleaned from the case histories described later. State funding, aimed at redistributing wealth, can be made available to organised groups of low-income people, thereby supplementing their own resources. Once in control of these resources, communities can select professional advice, designs and technologies to produce housing to their own specifications. This housing will 'fit' them because it is made for them. Management and maintenance will be less of a problem because residents themselves are organised and have the resources to deal with it.

A prerequisite of this developed form of popular control is the existence of community organisations that bring together users to define and assert their common needs and preferences in relation to those of other interest groups involved in the housing process. These organisations exist all over the world in a variety of forms and in different degrees of development. Empirical observation shows marked similarities in them, such as:

– They are collective solutions to common housing problems. People come together to finance, build and manage their own housing.

– They develop or find methods and technologies that are appropriate to their aims.

– The experience of housing themselves results in a strengthening of the community, which allows them to tackle other common needs and have a greater say in their society.

Subsidy, professional services, modern technologies, integration into official housing policies are not *necessarily* inimical to popular control of housing, but, applied correctly, can actually enable it. Ivan Illich has warned that even self-help is not safe from appropriation by professionals:

> The professional dream of rooting each hierarchy of needs in the grassroots goes under the banner of self-help. At present it is promoted by the new tribe of experts in self-help who have replaced the international development experts of the sixties. The professionalisation of laymen is their aim.

Illich goes on to describe how an American professor of architecture was taken to see a Mexican shanty town by a local colleague. He proceeded to take 'hundreds of rolls of pictures' of the various building techniques that held the settlement together:

> The pictures were analysed in Cambridge [at the Massachusetts Institute of Technology] and by the end of the year, new-baked US specialists in community architecture were busy teaching the people of Ciudad Netzahualcoyotl their problems, needs and solutions.

It would be ironic if we were to accept that the present crop of 'experts' in community architecture and self-help housing are in a better position to define what people want and need, than people themselves. Or that the 'experts' in appropriate technology are in a better position than the future users to decide what level of technology to use.

The following chapters will go on to explain why, in my view, community architecture is what people design themselves, with the benefit of professional advice; why appropriate technology is what people choose or develop for themselves, after having access to the range of possibilities open to them; and that the only ideal forms of organisation or finance are those which people voluntarily choose, on the basis of having control of the resources, and the necessary information and freedom to use those resources in the most appropriate way. Readers will determine whether the final result is 'enabling' or 'disabling'.

3 | The British context

Britain was probably one of the first Western societies to realise that the free market would not provide for everyone's needs. Under the Elizabethan Poor Laws, Boards of Guardians were set up to 'oversee' the poor, set local taxes to subsidise their income, and put them to work. According to Jane and Roy Darke in *Who Needs Council Housing?*:

> Out of this grew the workhouse system, with a regime deliberately made as unattractive as possible to discourage use of the facility, an attitude that persists in the treatment of the homeless today.

The 1800s brought a sweeping tide of industrialisation that depleted the rural areas and transformed many quaint old towns into sprawling, overcrowded urban centres. The population of London multiplied seven times during the century, and the population of Newcastle, for example, doubled in 40 years. But whereas employment, at least in periods of boom, was available in the cities, housing was scarce. The resulting conditions were similar to those of Third World cities today. As Engels saw it:

> In the houses one seldom sees a wooden or a stone floor, while the doors and windows are nearly always broken and badly fitting. And as for the dirt! Everywhere one sees heaps of refuse, garbage and filth. There are stagnant pools instead of gutters, and the stench alone is so overpowering that no human being, even partially civilised, would find it bearable to live in such a district.

Although some degree of 'self-build' was probably imported from the rural areas, most housing construction seems to have been the initiative of small investors. A few large employers built houses for their workers, sometimes setting up trusts for this purpose, but building finance came mainly from wealthy professionals – solicitors for example – who invested in housing for rent. This investment offered small but fairly regular returns, and better investment opportunities were not yet available. The housing thus provided reflects the drive to maximise profits, irrespective of the conditions created: 'single ends' in Scotland, and 'single apartments' in England, crammed families into single rooms; 'cellar dwellings' provided insanitary, underground accommodation; the 'court-houses' or 'back-to-backs' (many of which survive today) crowded families into airless, lightless warrens. Sanitary facilities were almost always lacking. According to an account of the day, houses were 'packed together in disorderly confusion in impudent defiance of all reasonable principles of town planning'.

The first timid beginnings of municipal intervention came in the mid-1800s. Powers were given to municipal authorities to close and demolish 'unfit' housing. These powers were also used to remove those communities that were in the way of transport or commercial development. Since no provision was made for the rehousing of those displaced by clearances, housing conditions actually deteriorated through these interventions, due to increased sub-division of existing dwellings and overcrowding.

By the end of the century the plight of the urban poor had reached crisis proportions, demonstrated in violent incidents like Bloody Sunday, 1887. Municipal authorities came under growing pressure, not only to regulate the private sector, but also to provide housing for the 'labouring classes'. In 1888, county and county borough councils were set up, including the London County Council, which pioneered municipal housing. In 1890 the Housing of the Working Classes Act gave local authorities broad powers to provide homes, primarily for skilled workers displaced by clearance. Although this Act laid the foundations for future council housing, production was initially slow. By 1914, the housing built by local authorities only accounted for 2 per cent of the country's total stock. The private rented sector provided 88 per cent of dwellings, and owner occupation a mere 10 per cent.

The non-government alternative to the private sector during this time were the great housing trusts (such as the Peabody Trust) which had the advantage of capital backing, allowing them to buy land and build for rent in spite of inflating prices. But their contribution was small, and by 1875 they had only housed 33,000 people. Occasional self-build ventures were also undertaken by building tradesmen, who could require payment in land from the gentry for services rendered. They could then build by exchanging services with fellow craftsmen, under the 'blood for blood' system.

1914-1945

Early municipal legislation had established the basis for council housing on the 'sanitary' principle. This meant that provision was primarily for the victims of slum clearance, and only to the most basic standards. The private sector was still expected to cater for the majority of low-income people. The realism of this principle was questionable, in view of the degradation of the slums and the social unrest it was producing. During the First World War, the Admiralty and the War Office had taken the unprecedented step of providing 11,000 homes for its heroes, and in 1915 a major rent strike in Glasgow forced the introduction of rent controls. Two years later a Royal Commission on Housing (the Hunter Committee) released a proposal suggesting that money should be borrowed interest-free from government to provide 'cottage housing' as an alternative to private slums. The post-war coalition government led by Lloyd George integrated these ideas into the radical Addison Act of 1919. This imposed on municipal authorities the duty to house the working classes generally, not only those displaced by clearance; it also allowed them to keep these properties under ownership rather than to sell them, as earlier legislation had required. This Act was based on an earlier document, called the Walters Report, which put forward an idyllic model of municipal 'garden cities', based on the building of quality homes with gardens – an ideal of what council housing ought to be. The housing was to be available at low rents, and caring, accountable local authorities would provide administration and maintenance. The Addison Act accounted for the building of 170,000 new council homes, at the same time as the national deficit was estimated at 800,000.

But the 'tug-of-war', that was to become a permanent feature of British housing, was poised to begin: in 1921, faced with spiralling building costs, subsidies to council house building were removed. The retreat helped undermine the government's credibility, and the Conservatives took power, with a marked dislike for the whole idea. Their alternative was to finance private builders through a 'flat rate' support system. They also supported owner-occupation by lowering interest rates on private loans. Helped by generous subsidy, the ownership of building land passed from the hands of the traditional gentry into those of developers and financiers. This was a boom period for the private builder, and 362,700 subsidised private sector dwellings were built under the Chamberlain Act of 1923.

In 1924, the first Labour government was formed, and immediately re-established the importance of council housing with the Wheatley Act. This inspired piece of legislation sponsored the building of some of the best municipal housing seen to date (to the garden city model): in the next three years over half a million houses were built, primarily in well-designed, well-built estates. But this provision was not for the poorest families, who were excluded from this fine housing by relatively high rents. To reach them with this method would have required even greater subsidies.

In 1930, in the wake of international financial collapse, the subsidies provided by the Wheatley Act were abandoned. In their place, the Greenwood Act offered a modest fixed subsidy, on the basis of each family rehoused from a clearance area, with a small addition to relieve overcrowding. This of course led to lowered standards and increased densities, not to mention repetitive designs. Council housing in the 1930s became ghetto housing, stigmatised by officials and tenants alike. But even then, some socialists, like George Orwell, continued to see them as positive collectivising influences.

On the other hand, private mortgages were now available from investment held back during the depression. There was a marked increase in owner-occupation by those who could afford it, fuelled by the stigma of council housing.

From 1919 to 1940 a total of 1,111,700 dwellings were built by local authorities, primarily under the Wheatley Act of 1924. The private sector, during the same period, built 2,886,000 homes, nearly half a million of which received subsidy under the Chamberlain Act of 1923. But then most house building ground to a halt, and stopped altogether during the Second World War.

1945-1964

In *Whatever Happened to Council Housing?* Michael Foot noted:

To build good houses for poor people on a huge scale was something that had never been accomplished in modern industrialised societies.

Yet this was precisely what the post-war Labour government set out to do. With a toll of half a million homes destroyed, 3 million damaged and the house construction programme at a standstill, the Bevan Programme set out to provide 200,000 new homes every year. Whereas the speculative builder was not considered a 'plannable instrument' local authorities were. They were 'locally and democratically controlled' and therefore could ensure that housing went to those in greatest need. Higher subsidies were again available for general needs housing, and low-interest loans were made available to local authorities from the Public Works Loan Board. The definition of council housing as being 'for the working classes' was removed from the 1949 Housing Act, and socially mixed estates, built on garden city principles, were encouraged. Average house size was increased from 750 square feet (in the 1930s) to 1,055 square feet. Bevan, the minister responsible, insisted on high standards even if it meant building fewer houses:

> While we shall be judged in a year or two by the number of houses we build, we shall be judged in ten years' time by the type of houses that we build.

It was the short-term judgement, however, that led to the eventual scrapping of these policies in 1947. One of the conditions of the US Marshall Aid plan to Britain's ailing post-war economy was a major cut in the housing budget. This led to production falling short of targets, and a loss of confidence in Labour's housing policies. Although the 200,000 houses a year target was nearly reached, Labour's 'failure' was widely criticised, and contributed to the return of the Conservatives in 1951. The new government actually surpassed the number of houses built the previous year by Labour, but only by reducing the standards that Bevan had so vehemently defended, as a look at average council house areas for the period shows: in 1946, the area was 1,026 square feet, rising to 1,055 square feet in 1949. In 1952, this had shrunk to 947 square feet; and in 1959 it was down to 897 square feet.

Local authority interest rates were allowed to rise. If they wanted to keep building, councils were obliged to raise rents. Subsidies for general needs housing were reduced and, in 1956, practically abolished. Slum clearance was encouraged, as well as 'systems' building and high-rise flats, by special allowances. Owner-occupation was encouraged by 100 per cent council mortgages, and tax relief on interest payments. Sale of council houses was encouraged and restrictions on private-sector building lifted. Labour authorities were dismayed at what they saw as sabotage of their programmes, but there was little they could do about it. As a result of all this, private sector building surpassed public, from 1958 to 1967.

When Labour returned to power in 1964, it was no longer committed to exclusive support for municipal housing. That year's Housing Act encouraged local authority loans for home improvement, particularly within designated General Improvement Areas. Councils were also given powers of 'compulsory improvement'. The Housing Corporation was set up, in order to encourage and fund the development of housing associations. Almshouses and industrial housing trusts, as well the new 'non-profit' co-ownership societies, were brought together within a single framework which attempted to integrate them into government housing policy.

1964-1974

The new Labour policy attempted to balance support equally between the public and the private sector, and to create a 'third arm' of non-profit 'voluntary' housing bodies. The 1965 White Paper *The Housing Programme* even hinted at the need for a 'withering away' of the council housing sector, once it had achieved its aims. Half a million houses per year were to be produced under this programme, divided equally between private and public sectors. In achieving this objective, the government placed its faith in technology and the private construction industry. Industrial building systems seemed to provide the answer to all housing problems, and their use was maximised. From 1964 to 1972 about half of all local authority building consisted of high-rise blocks of flats. Many builders offered package deals if they were guaranteed continuous programmes to make their operations profitable. Side by side with high-rise building came the *blitzkrieg* approach to redevelopment, where established communities were wiped away at the stroke of a planner's pen, and dispersed into alien new estates. The situation escalated until the late 1960s, when opposition to these policies focused on the collapse of Ronan Point, where three people were killed and 80 trapped as a result of a small gas explosion that brought down a sustaining wall. This brought the high-rise boom to an abrupt end.

During this period an attempt was made to improve the conditions of finance for council house building, by subsidising interest rates on loans available to local authorities. This was combined with the introduction of the Parker-Morris standard for public housing, and the 'cost-yardstick' to limit expenditure. But since interest rates continued rising, making money scarce, the only option was to limit the number of houses being built. Councils were once again obliged to concentrate on slum clearance and the relief of overcrowding.

Controls over the private rented sector were also increased at that time, as a result of the unsavoury practices of slum landlords (notoriously, Rachman in London). The Rent Act of 1965 gave increased security for tenants and introduced 'fair rents', some say at the cost of a shrinking rented sector.

In 1968 a serious economic slump precipitated the cutting of a further £82 million from the housing budget, development programmes were abandoned, and only empty sites, or rows of empty houses, were left to remind us that they had ever existed. As a result of this cutback, the 1969 Housing Act shifted official policy from new building to rehabilitation. This would presumably be cheaper, and help absorb the empty, decaying properties that were now evident in growing numbers. Against this background, organised squatting became a growing activity, spreading from London boroughs like Southwark and Redbridge to most major cities in the country. Those early squatting campaigns led to many of the 'short-life housing' schemes of today. By 1970, council house building had dropped to 180,000 per year, and then to 107,000 in 1973 – below the 1919 level.

With the Conservatives in power again in 1972 an attempt was made to raise the rents of council tenants to private sector level, with the Housing Finance Act. This was fiercely resisted by tenants in some areas, to the point of turning on the more conciliatory Labour authorities, declaring rent strikes and fielding 'tenants' candidates', in opposition to Labour, at local elections. Within this climate, a new role was seen for what became known as the housing association movement. The origins of this heterogeneous movement can be traced back to the almshouses of the Middle Ages, encompassing the housing trusts of the Victorian period. In the 1960s they had been joined by professionally-led housing societies developing cost-rent, co-ownership housing for people on middle incomes.

Although the rehabilitation of older, inner-city stock was seen as one of the main ways of improving housing conditions, it did not seem viable for local authorities to carry out this task on their own. A proposal (which received all-party support) was then made for funding to be provided by local authorities to 'voluntary housing bodies', to allow them to carry out this task. This proposal was echoed by a number of campaigning and community organisations, including Shelter, the National Campaign for the Homeless. The move fostered the development of community-based housing associations and co-operatives, to repair and manage older housing on a local level, thus keeping communities together. Initiatives like these boosted the lacklustre housing association movement, giving it new impetus and roots in the community, and gave the National Federation of Housing Associations a more prominent national role.

1975 to today

Labour returned to power in 1974 even less committed to municipal housing. The 1974 Housing Act took support for housing associations further. The role of the Housing Corporation as banker to the associations was extended, and the Housing Association Grant system was set up. The movement was offered funding to provide an extra 40,000 dwellings per year.

Local authorities, on the other hand, saw even their rehabilitation budgets slashed. One reason given for this reduction was the massive loan debt accumulated in local authority borrowing for past programmes. In 1974/75, this figure stood at £1,126 million, only slightly less than the total housing budget for that year.

Increasingly, the public housing budget was used to support owner-occupation. By 1976, 30 per cent of all housing expenditure was thus committed, in the form of council mortgages, improvement grants and tax relief to home buyers. In 1977, a Labour Green Paper *Housing Policy, a Consultative Document* recommended support for a number of new 'shared ownership' tenures, as well as straightforward owner-occupation.

While the search for alternatives continued, a Conservative government was formed in 1979, and embarked on the most concentrated attack on council housing to date in the form of the 1980 Housing Act. Returning to early doctrines which regarded municipal provision as, at best, a necessary evil, the government limited capital expenditure (even that resulting from sale of council houses), reduced budgets and subsidies, forced the sale of council houses at reduced rates, and abandoned central assessment of housing needs. Municipalisation was banned and councils urged to build for sale, and to sell land on the open market.

Council building dropped to 36,000 in 1981 and there was no equivalent rise in private sector building. Unemployment in the construction industry rocketed (to 400,000 in 1984) and subsidy cuts resulted in rising rents. Concessions to owner-occupiers, particularly through tax relief on mortgage payments, were maintained. Local authority housing once again became stigmatised, catering for an ever narrower range of disadvantaged households.

Housing associations and co-operatives did not come under similar attack, although expenditure was cut in real terms. The main intervention in this sector has been ideological, attempting to substitute 'steps to home ownership' initiatives (such as improvement for sale, community leasehold, etc.) for fair rented housing, and enforcing on associations the tenant's Right to Buy.

The combination of cutbacks in public housing expenditure (only 26,600 council homes were built in 1985), tax relief on mortgages and the Right to Buy further stimulated a rise in owner-occupation. With it came a disproportionate rise in house prices in some areas, particularly in London, which made buying increasingly difficult for people with low incomes and for housing associations. Inflated prices, coupled with the decrease of public and housing association provision has prompted more people to take on mortgages they cannot afford, resulting in 11,000 repossessions by building societies in 1985, and even more registered and unregistered homelessness. There have also been numerous cases of local authorities having to buy back homes which have been bought under the Right to Buy but which tenants cannot afford to maintain. The situation is likely to deteriorate even further if the government fulfils its threat to cut payment of interest on mortgages for the unemployed.

By the end of 1985, with nearly 700,000 council dwellings sold, the Right to Buy bonanza seemed to have abated. An estimated 6 million people still live in council stock, and a recent DoE report indicated that this stock needs £20 billion spent on it to bring it into adequate repair, as well as £6 million a year on its maintenance. The government has little intention of footing this bill, and the 1986 Housing and Planning Act is aimed at obliging councils to dispose of existing stock – to private developers, to local management trusts, or to housing co-operatives formed by tenants.

If this last provision was intended to accentuate the breach between the advocates of municipal housing and the proponents of co-operatives, it has certainly succeeded. The Association of Metropolitan Authorities has accused co-operatives of being the 'gravediggers' of municipal housing for their support of the Act. The only major concession so far won is that tenants will be 'consulted' on whether management of the housing will go to private agencies or to co-ops. The viability of such 'enforced collectivisation' remains to be seen.

Homelessness – the great British failure

Although Britain does not have an identifiable 'informal' sector of people who fall outside both commercial and government provision, as poorer countries do, there is, however, an ever-growing section of people for whom no adequate provision is made by either of those two sectors, and who sometimes have to revert to 'illegal' solutions. They are usually referred to as 'the homeless', and conveniently placed into two categories: 'official' or 'priority' homeless (those for whom local authorities accept responsibility) and 'unofficial' or 'non-priority' homeless (those for whom they do not).

Until the advent of council housing, the private sector was supposed to provide for everyone's needs, and those who fell out were provided for by the Speenhamland Act and the Poor Laws through workhouses and similar institutions. After 1919, council housing was built for the better-paid working class. The rest had to make do with Poor Law provision, or had to take matters into the own hands, as in the mass occupation of a disused refugee camp by homeless families from Tyneside at this time. This situation continued throughout the 1930s and into the Second World War.

The 1945 Labour Government first noted the discrepancy in the provision of housing for different sections of low-income people, and attempted to redress it in the National Assistance Act of 1948.

Section 21 of this Act put on local authorities the responsibility to provide a roof over the head of anyone in their area who would otherwise be homeless. The post-war squatting movement, headed by an organisation of ex-servicemen called the Vigilantes, undoubtedly helped to accelerate this change, by encouraging the occupation of disused army camps by homeless people. By 1946, 40,000 people were said to living in these settlements.

To meet their obligations under the National Assistance Act, local authorities requisitioned old workhouses, army camps and police stations. This housing was not considered to be on the same level as council housing, and in fact was handled by a different department of the authority (Social Services rather than Housing), and funded from different budgets. Attitudes and practices were reminiscent of the Poor Laws. Fred Berry, in *Housing – The Great British Failure*, observes:

> Restricted contact between husband and wife, employment as wardens of authoritarian NCOs, the widespread acceptance of isolated and sub-standard accommodation was quite in order for such families, and the ultimate threat was of removing children into care.

This was the extent of official provision for a whole section of the community throughout the 1950s and 60s, when attention was nationally focused on it by the film *Cathy Come Home*, and the launching of Shelter, the National Campaign for the Homeless. General outcry was directed towards official treatment of the homeless, but little was done at that stage. In 1966, 2,500 families were placed in 'temporary accommodation' by local authorities, rising to 5,630 families in 1971. At the same time, two-thirds of people applying were turned down, so actual homelessness was probably much higher. In 1976, 50,000 applied for housing as homeless persons, of whom just over 18,000 were housed. The number of people in short-life housing also continued to grow, and an estimated 30,000 people were living in squats in London in 1971.

Because of limited budgets, it was no longer possible for local authorities to try to house all homeless persons directly. Charitable organisations, like the Salvation Army, were relied on, as well as bed-and-breakfast establishments. Because of pressure from different quarters, the 1977 Housing (Homeless Persons) Act was introduced, to reorganise and, it was hoped, improve the situation of homeless people. Although it provided local authorities with no extra funding to deal with the problem, the Act at least ironed out some of the most obvious ambiguities. Housing Departments were given responsibility for combatting homelessness, which at least gave families more access to permanent council stock, although they might have to go through the mill of temporary accommodation in the process. The measure, however, did not increase overall provision.

By 1981 157,000 families applied for housing as homeless persons. About half of these were housed, many in private bed-and-breakfast accommodation. Many of the people rejected by local authorities for housing also found their way into these establishments, thanks to the Department of Health and Social Security's 'board and lodgings' allowances, which allowed them to meet the inflated daily charges. By 1979 49,000 families were housed in bed-and-breakfast establishments and in receipt of board and lodgings allowances. By 1984 the figure had risen to 139,000 families. Conditions in this housing were described in *The Guardian* by the writer Salman Rushdie:

> The fire was at 46 Gloucester Place, owned by London Lets, whose proprietor is one Mr J. Doniger. When it started, no alarm rang. It had been switched off. The fire extinguishers were empty. The fire exits were blocked. It was night time, but the stairs were in darkness, because there were no bulbs in the lighting sockets. And in the single, cramped top floor room, where the cooker was next to the bed and where they had been housed for nine months, Mrs Abdul Krim, a Bangladeshi woman, and her five-year-old son and three-year-old daughter died of suffocation. They had been housed in London Lets by Camden Council at a cost that one Councillor estimated at £280 a week.

Bed-and-breakfast accommodation is the equivalent of the Victorian 'single apartment' with one difference: landlords now can have their exhorbitant charges met from public funds – at the same time as council building programmes are brought to a halt. In response to this criticism, the government recently tried to reduce the amount of, and eligibility to, board and lodgings payments, forcing

many thousands more out of bed-and-breakfast, only to have these
changes ruled illegal by the High Court. SHAC, the charity for the
homeless, has demonstrated that it would be cheaper (and better)
for the government to build directly than to continue paying out
huge sums to slum landlords. So far this recommendation has been
ignored.

In 1984 80,000 were accepted as homeless by local authorities,
and about the same number turned away. In 1985 it was 94,000,
a third of these in London. 'Official' and 'unofficial' homelessness
– bed-and-breakfast, council temporary accommodation, short-life
housing, squats, night shelters, sleeping rough – continues to rise.
If the government were brave enough to keep count (which they
are not) they would probably find that at least 200,000 households
fell into these categories by 1987 – appropriately declared
International Year of Shelter for the Homeless!

Summary

The housing needs of pre-industrial Britain were more or less met
by a combination of private landlords and traditional self-build
practices. Those who had access to neither had to rely on the Poor
Laws and the parish. With the Industrial Revolution, these methods
were no longer enough, due to the growth of cities and housing
need. Although capital was available to build housing for rent, the
general results were the Victorian slums, so reminiscent of the
shanty towns of today's Third World. Nonetheless, that provision
was enough to prevent the growth of a large, identifiable 'informal'
sector, such as we see in Third World cities today.

State intervention was precipitated by this sprawling, unplanned
growth. Municipal authorities were given powers to clear unfit
housing, to make way for transport and commercial development.
This in turn made housing problems greater through continued
demolition, and required even greater intervention in the form of
direct provision by municipal authorities for those displaced by
clearance. The apparatus was thus created for the development
of mass council housing in the next century.

Philanthropic trusts and self-help ventures (such as the 'blood
for blood' system) provided no real alternative during this time.
The former were limited by the commercial framework in which
they had to operate, and the latter by lack of capital and official
support.

The Labour movement of the 1920s achieved control of government and municipal authorities and attempted to use them to meet the housing needs of the working class. Large subsidies allowed local authorities to contract the building of good quality homes to private builders, who built to 'ideal' designs and standards. This housing could now be kept in the ownership of local authorities, who now became public landlords of growing importance. But subsidies were never high enough to fulfil the expectations created, and so even the best Labour administrations appeared to fail in their aims. This allowed Conservatives to repeatedly take over the apparatus of working-class housing, which they usually operated in the way most likely to undermine the public sector and support the private. Although councils were proud of their 'democracy and accountability' through local elections, the result often put the management of low-income housing into the hands of people who were far from sympathetic to this provision. This, added to growing financial constraints, both internal and external, from the 1930s till today, has made the performance of council housing erratic and disappointing during its first 70 years.

The main achievement of council housing has been to take over the role of the private landlord for most of the low-income sector. This role has been vital and provided many millions of people with adequate housing for many years. The main shortcomings, however, have been: to produce housing that is often inappropriate to people's needs and preferences; to fail to develop flexible, responsive, community-based management and maintenance techniques; and to fail to provide for many of those who are poorest and in greatest need.

One of the endemic distortions of the housing debate in Britain has been to see it as an uncompromising clash between two exclusive models. Thus Labour has traditionally favoured the channelling of subsidies to municipal authorities to build a large public rented sector under council control. Conservatives, on the other hand, have favoured using whatever limited subsidies can be made available to support private home ownership, and private rental to provide for the poorest. All other housing possibilities are regarded as 'steps to private ownership' by both camps. The possibility of any 'intermediate' community ownership or control has been usually ignored.

Over the last 20 years, however, Labour has shown itself

increasingly uncertain about the municipal housing model, and has flirted with various alternatives. This search, however, has not been based on any clear analysis of the problem, and has culminated in the adoption of policies that are sometimes indistinguishable from those of the Conservatives. Only recently has the possibility of council provision being based on some form of community control been seriously raised, although this might be the ultimate way to prevent a 'hijacking' of public resources by private interests, such as we have seen with the Conservative government, and their eventual privatisation. Matters are further confused by the recent Liberal/SDP move to seize the housing 'middle ground', e.g. favouring housing co-ops and community-based associations, at the same time as more doctrinaire Labour councils embark on traditional mass council housing programmes in the face of government sanctions. More confusion was added by the government's attempt to bring in council tenants' co-ops to support the privatisation initiatives in the new Housing and Planning Act. Resolving the apparent contradiction between municipal provision of housing and community self-management and control is still a challenge for the future.

4 | Self-help in Bristol

Bristol has roots dating back to prehistoric and Roman times, but its history begins in the Middle Ages, when a trading settlement was founded on the junctions of the rivers Avon and Frome. From this convenient position came its name: 'bridge-place'. The village offered commercial and military advantages, and both were exploited from an early age. By the 11th century, Bristol was shipping slaves to Ireland. The Norman conquerors turned it into a fort, which they held throughout most of the period. They did not, however, interfere with the trading activities of its inhabitants, which brought the town growing wealth and influence.

In the 1500s, the powerful Bristol Merchant Venturers' Society succeeded in establishing a monopoly of overseas trade through the port, by means of a Royal Charter. Cloth of all descriptions was exported, in exchange for fruits, spices, wool, tobacco and sugar. Ports of call included Ireland, Europe, Iceland and Africa. The quest for new markets spurred John Sebastian Cabot to land on the North American mainland in 1497.

The fortunes of this group were further favoured by the new Parliament's decision to exclude Irish merchants from access to the colonies. With their foreign competitors crushed, only London rivalled the success of Bristol merchants.

In spite of its relatively small size (20,000 inhabitants in 1700, in contrast to London's 750,000) Bristol became the country's second city. Much of the wealth thus concentrated found its way into the city's stately architecture, particularly in the wealthy Redland, Clifton and Cotham areas. But poverty was also evident, and a 1696 'Act for the Erecting of Hospitals and Workhouses' concentrated the administration of parish Poor Laws into one central authority.

From the early 1700s the Merchant Venturers challenged London's Royal Africa Company for control of the thriving slave

27

trade. In 1725 Bristol shipped 17,000 slaves to the New World, compared to London's 26,000. But in 1771 Bristol outstripped London, by sending 8,810 slaves, crammed in the lower decks of merchant ships, to London's 8,136. Both were soon overtaken by young Liverpool, which by 1800 had a virtual monopoly of the slave trade. The wise merchants of Bristol then shifted their attention to other products, like sugar, which also provided the basis for local industries like distilleries and confectioners.

Bristol's success in trading was partly responsible for its lagging behind in the Industrial Revolution. Merchant wealth went into sumptuous housing, but little of it found its way into new industries. What was worse, much of the city's population earned a living through hand manufacture of shoes and clothing, and people were made destitute by the influx of industrially produced goods from other cities. Nonetheless, the population continued growing throughout the Industrial Revolution, reaching 360,000 by 1901. But by this time Bristol was no longer the second city, having been overtaken by industrial centres like Birmingham, Manchester and Leeds.

Urbanisation without much industrial growth brought declining social conditions. In 1840 observers remarked on the festering houses in the centre of the city, the stench of effluent which saturated the banks of the Avon, and the mortality rates surpassed only by Liverpool and Manchester. A survey of the time showed that one-third of a sample of working families interviewed were destitute, and half were living in one room or less. At the same time the building of expensive housing continued, and an 1882 Royal Commission on Working Class Housing noted the many empty houses in more expensive parts of the city.

The end of the century brought a new wave of industrialisation, with firms like W.D. & H.O. Wills (tobacco), J.S. Fry (chocolate) and E.A. & O. Robinson (confectioners). These new industries provided some extra employment for the city's impoverished population, breaking the stranglehold that merchant capital had long had on the city's economy. Even so, resistance to change was strong, and the Merchant Venturers succeeded in delaying reforms like the provision of public gas and water, through their opposition to 'municipal trading'. By the turn of the century, such reforms were inevitable, and Bristol's municipal housing provision developed on much the same model as other major cities. With the growth of the trade union movement and the Labour Party, Bristol Corporation became a typical council housing authority, suffering the many ups and downs of government policy over the years, eventually building up a stock of 45,000 council homes, less than a third of the city's total.

Bristol in the 1970s

In 1971, Bristol had a population of 427,000, which seemed to be slowly declining. Unemployment in the south-west was not particularly high in relation to other parts of England (10.8 per cent of the working population), and much lower than in parts of the north. This unemployment was probably concentrated in the urban areas, especially in Bristol.

Due to public housing cutbacks and the continuing shrinking of the private rented sector, growing homelessness became apparent in the 1970s. In 1971, the Joint Working Party on Homelessness in the Counties of Gloucester, Somerset and Bristol, reported that 44 families and 157 homeless single people had been accepted for housing under the 1948 National Assistance Act. Since it was usual at that time for Social Services Departments to turn down two-thirds of applicants, it is likely that many more people were without a roof over their heads at that time.

Simultaneously, the number of empty houses dotted throughout the city grew. Some were empty as a result of abortive public development projects; some were privately owned, empty because of disrepair or for speculative reasons. The total number was a matter for conjecture. Ron Bailey, in his timely book *The Homeless and the Empty Houses*, noted:

> The examination of empty property has so far shown two things: firstly, that large numbers of houses get lost or somehow disappear from statistics, and secondly, that large numbers of houses are lost or destroyed years in advance of redevelopment plans, and thus disappear without a trace from official information.

Independent surveys carried out by Shelter (1972-73) and Self-Help Community Housing Association (SCHA) – for which I worked – showed something like 1,000 empty houses in inner Bristol, their ownership divided roughly into the following categories:

Private. These numbered about 450 and were sometimes empty for years, presumably awaiting sale or repair. Some were the subject of closing orders.

Public. These numbered about 400, and usually belonged to Bristol Corporation (later passed on to Avon County Council). Some belonged to the university, the Water Board or other public bodies. They were usually awaiting sale, demolition or repair, sometimes many years.

Housing associations. These only became common after the Housing Act of 1974 supported housing association rehabilitation projects. They were properties bought by associations in order to repair and let. They could be standing up to two years awaiting the necessary approvals. Throughout the city there could be as many as 200 at any one time.

To many people, it seemed absurd that homelessness was growing at the same time as so many houses were potentially usable and standing empty.

Municipal response

For some time, Bristol Corporation had been dominated by a fairly chauvinist Labour Group, mostly 'conservative' trade unionists and academics, who felt called upon to protect the city's municipal heritage against unwanted 'foreign' elements. Thus provision for homelessness was limited and uninviting, and acceptance onto the waiting list for council housing was conditional on meeting a long list of requirements: e.g. having been already resident in the city for more than five years, never having been evicted for rent arrears, never having squatted, etc. The introduction of the Housing (Homeless Persons) Act of 1977 changed this somewhat by making homelessness the direct responsibility of the Housing Department, and giving people qualifying under this Act access to the permanent housing stock. But even then, access was strictly limited, and would usually only take place after families had spent several months in inadequate temporary accommodation. Nonetheless, in 1981 alone, 356 families were accepted as homeless by the council under these provisions.

Discriminatory attitudes among councillors and top council staff towards the homeless and unemployed were frequently evident to anyone working in the area. One top civil servant, at a meeting which I attended on behalf of SCHA, described our tenants as 'the scum of mankind'. Attitudes like these made co-operation with the council very difficult until the late 1970s, when the hold of 'traditional' Labour was broken by a younger, more radical element sympathetic to minorities and community organisations. This reflected the national and local transformation of the Labour Party.

There were other political influences in Bristol at the time, but they were relatively unimportant in council politics until the formation of Avon County Council, when many empty properties in Bristol were transferred to the ruling Conservative group and remained empty for years.

Action on homelessness

The introduction of short-life housing into Bristol was preceded by an outburst of militant squatting, first focused on the organised occupation (in 1972) of four Georgian houses being held empty by a London-based developer. The squatters, mainly young single people, were not so much motivated by their need for a home, as by their determination to publicise the growing plight of the homeless and the scandal of empty properties. They called upon Bristol Corporation to expropriate these and similar properties under the 1957 Housing Act, and to use them for housing. The Labour Housing Committee was not sympathetic. They rejected the call, stating that privately owned properties had nothing to do with them, and called upon the government to make squatting a criminal offence. The possibility of council/community co-operation on homelessness did not appear likely at this point.

In 1973, as a result of cutbacks to the University Grants Committee budget, Bristol went through a student housing crisis. Hundreds of university and polytechnic students found themselves homeless at the beginning of term, and in the mood of activism of the time, were prepared to contemplate many forms of direct action. A group of homeless students formed a society in the university union, known as Students' Community Housing. Members of this organisation occupied 11 properties under the ownership of the University and the Bristol United Hospitals. Rooms not occupied by students in these properties were given over to homeless non-students, and a basic organisation, based on weekly meetings to make collective decisions, was formed.

Negotiations through the students' union allowed this occupation

to continue for over a year, giving the group time to consolidate its organisation. At a general meeting, a decision was taken to form a legal body that would allow the housing group access to official resources. With the help of the London-based Family Squatting Advisory Service (now called the Advisory Service for Squatters), the group was registered as a housing association with charitable rules under the 1965 Industrial and Provident Society's Act. In taking this step, members agreed on several common objectives:
1. To actually provide housing for homeless people, not just to campaign around the issue.
2. To secure housing for other homeless people, not just for those who had initiated the organisation.
3. To operate on the basis of an 'open' structure, allowing new applicants for housing as well as existing members to participate in the weekly meetings.
4. To rely primarily on those resources available to members (self-help, voluntary contributions) rather than on government sponsorship, but at the same time to pursue any public resources available.

Accepting the charitable housing association rules entailed a minimal structuring of the organisation: a secretary had to be elected to deal with paperwork; a treasurer to collect membership fees and voluntary contributions, and pay bills; a management committee (nominal at this point) whose names could be submitted in returns to the Registrar.

At this stage the structure was on paper rather than in practice. Almost everything still operated on a collective informal level. Since the association was not yet legally in possession of any properties, it assumed the role of a squatting advice service. Homeless people, referred by professional housing bodies, would be told where empty houses were and how to occupy them without breaking the law. They would later return for advice on how to carry out repairs, how to negotiate 'licences to occupy' with owners, and so on.

In order to give this advice, association organisers relied on their own experience and on information available from established London groups – contained in publications like *The Squatters' Handbook* and *The Squatters' Repair Manual*. Within two years a wealth of common wisdom in these matters had been built up, which was put to good use in the following period of 'legality'.

Self-Help Community Housing Association

In 1975, two years after the University occupations, and a year after its formation as a legal body, SCHA received its first licence for the use of an empty property, owned by Bristol United Hospitals. This property had been previously squatted and the hospital authorities were persuaded that SCHA could repair and manage the property at its own expense, returning it vacant in two years time if a licence agreement was entered into to allow them to occupy it. A licence arrangement was suggested (rather than a tenancy), because it did not require rent to be paid to the hospital, and granted no security of tenure to the occupier. It was merely 'permission to occupy' a dwelling for a limited period of time. This arrangement, essential for short-life housing, was in fact a loophole in the Rent Acts. When private landlords tried later to exploit this arrangement, legislation on licences was tightened up.   Another aspect of the licence agreement was that although no rent was paid by the association to the owner, the association could legally charge a 'licence fee' to the occupiers of the property. This licence fee could be equivalent to a current rental and would be honoured by the Department of Health and Social Security for the purposes of Rent Allowance. A system of self-financing initial repairs was set up on this basis, where an initial loan secured to repair the property was repaid on the basis of these licence fees. These repairs, initially, were to a minimum level and carried out by volunteers.

Properties thus repaired were allocated at the weekly general meetings, and everyone was invited to vote on who should live in them. In practice, these were usually people living in squats or who had been referred to the Association as homeless. The occupiers were required to sign a simple licence agreement with the association, where they agreed to keep the premises in a fit state, to pay a weekly rent (licence fee) and to move out on a pre-arranged date. The rent on the first property was set at £2 per week per room, considerably lower than an equivalent rent for a private dwelling. Later this payment was increased to Fair Rent level, and became the basis for most repair, management and maintenance operations of the association.

SCHA had a dual role – formal and informal – during this time: it managed a tiny number of properties under legal licence agreements, repaired them and collected rents, but simultaneously co-ordinated a loosely-knit 'federation' of squats around the city, and acted as an unofficial referral centre for homeless people looking for squats.

This situation changed from 1976 onwards as a result of an agreement between Solon (South-West) Housing Association and SCHA. As a result of the increased funding made available to Housing Corporation-registered housing associations under the 1974 Housing Act, Solon had acquired a number of properties that were then in the pipeline for conversion. These properties, like other empty houses in Bristol, were the target of 'scrappers' – scavengers for metal – and vandals. Solon was eventually persuaded to hand these houses over to SCHA on a temporary licence basis. Gradually, about 50 properties were made over, and basic repairs were carried out using the accumulated rent income. These properties were mainly used to rehouse people who had previously been living in squats, so occupiers were expected to deal with non-skilled repairs themselves. As rental income built up, however, individual members began to specialise in carrying out on a casual basis different works – like electrical wiring, plumbing, book-keeping, and rent-collecting – sometimes having their expenses met from rental income.

Professional self-help

One consequence of its informal style of operation during the first few years was SCHA's dependence on voluntary and casual labour to carry out most of its work. This continued to be the case until 1980, in spite of the fact that for the last three years it had been managing 80-100 houses at any one time, repairing and handing back about 50-60 houses every year.

This informality had a high price. Rent arrears were astronomical, easily accounting for half the possible rental income. Repairs, especially maintenance, depended on occupiers being able to do the work themselves, which was unrealistic, particularly in view of the growing number of homeless families without squatting experience who were being housed. Some sort of 'professionalisation', both of administrative and building functions, was called for, in order to improve conditions, and in turn, reduce rent arrears.

This professionalisation took place gradually, almost unintentionally. At first, small builders had been used to carry out initial repairs, but neither costs nor results were satisfactory. A small in-house repair team was set up, formed by members who had or were willing to acquire the necessary building skills. These members in turn became very involved in the running of the organisation.

Similar professionalisation took place in administration and financial control. Because it was a Friendly Society, the association's books had to be audited yearly, so a book-keeper had to keep detailed records of rental payments and expenditure for presentation to the association's auditor. Members in persistent arrears were visited by 'tenancy workers' who tried to help them solve their financial problems. On the whole, it was members with some academic or previous relevant work experience who took on these professional roles.

Permanent property

Attempts were made from an early stage to acquire permanent properties collectively, in order to meet more than just the temporary housing needs of members. This first took the form (in 1975) of an application for registration with the Housing Corporation. If registration had been successful it would have given SCHA access to Housing Association Grant (HAG) which would have enabled it to purchase and convert older properties or to build housing for its members. The first application was rejected, re-presented and rejected again in 1979. The final reason given was that the association had connections with squatting, and was therefore unfit to handle public funds.

The Housing Corporation's refusal to register SCHA left it one alternative for acquiring permanent property, and that was to seek private mortgage funding. But there were misgivings among both staff and membership as to the wisdom of this move, since a considerable financial commitment would have to be undertaken for relatively little extra housing. A pilot project to secure mortgage funding for a property from the Abbey National Building Society (in 1982) fell through when the association's bid was 'gazumped' by a private builder while waiting for planning permission for conversion. After that, the idea of mortgage funding was subsequently dropped as complicated and unrealistic. Later hopes were rekindled by the council's granting of 30-year leases on two houses, in effect permanent housing. Long-term management of council-owned stock might in fact provide a less expensive form of permanent housing for SCHA.

Subsidy

Another effect of the Housing Corporation's refusal to register SCHA was to deny it direct access to the Corporation's 'Mini-HAG' grant – a subsidy for the provision of short-life housing by registered associations, which provides a basic level of repair according to the life of the property. At present about £3,000 can be obtained for a property with two to four years' life. SCHA was able to get round this block on the basis of its good relations with Solon Housing Association. A 'development agreement' was drawn up, where Solon agreed to license and repair the properties with the grant in the first instance, and then hand them over to the short-life group for management and maintenance. This arrangement allowed several long-term empty properties owned by public bodies to be brought into use, until 1982 when the government restricted the use of Mini-HAG. As a result, in 1983 no properties in Bristol were repaired with this grant and only recently, with the relaxation of restrictions, Mini-HAG has become available again.

Repairs on properties renovated with this grant were initially carried out by a building co-operative, set up for this purpose by members of SCHA. The co-operative contracted the work from Solon, whose in-house architectural team would draw up basic specifications for the work. Works under these arrangements were more thorough than those previously carried out by by volunteers but were still very much based on self-help repair principles, involving cheap, quick, simple techniques, which used recycled materials wherever possible.

A typical job might involve the felting of roofs, replacement of window frames and doors, replastering of walls, a damp-course, the replacement of some floor and roof joists and floorboards (often due to dry rot), replacement of ceilings, and maybe the building of internal partition walls, as well as the inevitable rewiring and replumbing. This work was not that different from repair work currently carried out by small contractors for home improvement grants. The fact that a 'non-professional' co-operative of SCHA members was carrying this work out caused some unease in Labour circles, but this was eventually overcome by their joining a union (the TGWU) and working for union rates.

Over the years, the members of the co-operative and the repair teams which followed it succeeded in developing an 'appropriate technology' for carrying out quick, cheap repairs, which allowed them to bring back into use hundreds of properties that would otherwise have stayed empty. When the building co-operative or other specialised teams were not available to carry out this work, private builders were used at a higher cost and with less satisfactory results.

Staffing

In 1980, as a result of the increased work-load and extra commitments involved in the handling of Mini-HAG properties, SCHA applied to the Housing Association Charitable Trust (HACT) for a grant to fund the wages of a full-time co-ordinator. This application was successful, and small central offices were set up in the front room of one of the new properties. The new staff group included a co-ordinator (myself), who looked after general administration and carried out some repairs; a part-time treasurer, who kept books and financial records (including rent records); and a rent collector, who visited all licensed properties. A number of members also formed part of a casual repair team, who carried out initial repair and some maintenance works, and were paid on an hourly basis.

Financial improvement became evident in SCHA's 1980-81 Annual Report: rental income rose to nearly £19,000 per year, without a significant increase in the number of properties held at any one time. The level of repair and maintenance carried out by the association remained relatively low, since only slightly more than £3,000 was spent on direct building costs that year. Improved operations had the effect of bettering the group's image and pre-conversion properties were soon offered by two other major housing associations in the area. This did not, however, lead to a considerable increase in the number of properties used, since it coincided with cutbacks in funding. Pre-conversion properties at the time represented 75 per cent of SCHA's housing stock. At present, the figure is about 60 per cent, the rest being long-term empty houses owned by public bodies.

At this point, it is worth noting the absurdity of current government restrictions on the use of empty properties by housing associations, and the funding of their repair, in contrast with the apparent acceptance (if not encouragement) of extortionate bed-and-breakfast alternatives. Examples are plentiful: the restrictions on the use of Mini-HAG to houses intended for demolition in 1982;

the creation of security of tenure for licensees in local authority-owned properties (under the 1980 Housing Act); and more recently (in February 1987), the 'illegalising' by John Patten, then Minister for Housing, of a whole host of arrangements developed by local authorities to support short-life schemes. What are these restrictions achieving, apart from creating more misery for hundreds of homeless people who will not be able to use these properties as temporary homes? I suppose that, with doctrinaire logic, they do prevent local authorities from using short-life properties as a way of providing 'public sector' temporary housing for those in need, in the face of continuing cuts, which, unlike bed-and-breakfast accommodation, is through a partnership with non-profit community groups. Clearly private enterprise and the profit-motive must be protected in the face of such attacks.

Internal organisation

By 1981, the structure of SCHA had also changed. Under pressure from the Housing Corporation, which was not entirely happy with SCHA's growing use of properties repaired with the aid of Mini-HAG, Solon carried out a Monitoring Report on the short-life group, which attempted to identify inadequacies in its structure and procedures. One of the main criticism was SCHA's system of 'open democracy', through which all decisions were made. It was considered unsuitable for the serious legal and financial responsibilities which the group was undertaking. Solon recommended instead that control be centralised in an elected management committee, which could supervise all the operations of the association. Consultation with the membership could continue taking place at general meetings but these would not be as frequent and would only discuss broader policy issues. They also recommended increased professionalisation of key functions, such as accounting, rent collection, tenancy work and repairs. The structure suggested was in many ways a mirror image of Solon itself.

These changes were put into effect as a condition of further access to Mini-HAG. Although in theory the management committee structure was still democratic, there was some misgiving that the substitution of a small management group for open meetings of members and new applicants might 'close' the association in many ways. Although the weekly general meetings were sometimes chaotic, they at least allowed ordinary members and applicants a say in the running of the organisation. With this new structure, basic decisions (including allocation) would become the responsibility of a handful of people who could take them without involving members, while the general meetings would become more of a social event, with little decision-making power. Power, which had before been diffused, would now be concentrated.

The validity of these misgivings was evident in the notable decline in participation that followed re-structuring. New tenants saw the committee as landlords, who were providing them with housing and were responsible for all problems arising. Few newcomers were prepared to elbow their way into the apparently exclusive management committee. Gradually, reliance on self-help, so apparent in the early days of the organisation, was lost and replaced by a dependence on money, to pay for the professional services to get the various jobs done.

A further step in this direction was taken with the extension of the revenue grant into the 1981-82 period. Staffing was expanded to include a maintenance co-ordinator, a book-keeper, three tenancy workers and a part-time repair team, again without any significant increase in the number of properties held. Improved management and higher rent levels raised the income for the period to nearly £30,000 in 1981-82, and expenditure on repairs to £9,500 in that year.

The MSC – and related programmes

In 1982-83 a further financial boost was received, in the shape of the Manpower Services Commission (MSC)'s 'Community Enterprise Programme' (CEP). This was a job-creation programme for the long-term unemployed, which allowed the payment of wages ranging from £89 to £110 per week, on the basis of a grant paid by the Commission. Under this programme SCHA secured wages for five full-time administrative workers, which completely subsidised the wages bill. Rents could now be used for initial repairs, maintenance and management overheads. Rental income, without a substantial increase in stock, mainly on the basis of improved rent collection, rose to nearly £50,000 for 1982-83, and the repairs bill to £15,000. Conditions in properties were now much better, and a small repair team was employed on a permanent part-time basis.

Also through the CEP scheme, SCHA participated in the setting up of a skilled building team, to carry out initial repair works on longer-term empty properties. This team, operating under the auspices of a community organisation known as Community Workforce to which SCHA was affiliated, used both Mini-HAG and other loan funds to repair a number of properties for use as short-life housing.

The CEP programme was curtailed in 1983, and the programme brought in to replace it – the Community Programme (CP) – was considered unacceptable in many circles, particularly by the unions. SCHA staff blacked it (against the wishes of the management committee) because it did not allow for the re-employment of existing staff, and because the rates offered were below the union minimum. Considering this as a vote of no confidence, the management committee resigned en masse, shifting the balance of power within the association. Ever since the implementation of Solon 'control by committee' recommendations, there had been a decline in participation by ordinary tenants. By the time of the conflict around CP, the committee was little more than an unrepresentative group of 'old hands', who had no real support from the ordinary members, who saw themselves as just tenants. Staff numbers, on the other hand, were growing, and there was a strong collective consciousness, especially as far as working conditions, rates of pay, and self-management were concerned. By rejecting the CP proposal staff asserted that their own interests as workers were at least as important as the ulterior aims of the organisation. The position of the association thus shifted even further in the direction of 'worker-control' (rather than 'user-control') having passed through an intermediate phase of 'control by management committee'.

The loss of MSC funding also brought on a temporary financial crisis, with little money for wages. The association pinned its hopes on getting the support of Bristol Council Labour Group for an application to the DoE for Urban Aid. Thanks to their good relations with the new radical Labour group and the support of other community organisations, SCHA was able to secure funding for the wages of a basic administrative staff over a five-year period. Staff, some of whom were now on the dole, were re-employed. But the situation was not totally solved. The introduction of the Unified Housing Benefit caused further losses of rental income, due to delays in implementation and mishandling by the local authority. Once this situation was stabilised, the association attempted to secure a further Urban Aid Grant to pay for the wages of a full-time building team. This application was rejected by the DoE (who thought it sounded too much like direct labour) and the association then had to continue relying on part-time, casual employment of builders and maintenance staff. In 1985 the application was re-submitted and was successful, with the result that SCHA now have a direct labour section.

Community development

Throughout its existence, SCHA has promoted and supported several community projects and activities, not always related directly to housing. These have included the regular printing of a news-sheet, the organisation of concerts, outings, social events, photographic exhibitions and film shows, as well as several community enterprises such as a removal service and a building co-operative. SCHA also supported the setting up of four local housing co-operatives (at least two of which were eventually registered with the Housing Corporation and secured permanent housing) and of a separate short-life organisation in Bath. Recently, a child-care organiser has been employed (under the DHSS Opportunities for Volunteers scheme), to promote social activities for tenants, and especially for their children during school holidays. These are important aspects of the work of the SCHA, and have contributed to the development of community spirit in the city over the years.

Value for money

By 1983-84 rental income had shot up to an all-time high of £65,000. This sum represented about 60 per cent of the association's income, the rest being made up of grants, donations, loans and other income from commercial building work. Public subsidy (in the form of Urban Aid and Housing Corporation allowances) amounted to about 20 per cent of income. Expenditure on repairs carried out by the association remained at £15,000 during the year, and most of this work was carried out directly by SCHA's repair team. The number of houses under management throughout that year fluctuated between 70 and 90, which is more or less average for any year, but was perhaps growing to higher than average as the number of longer-term short-life properties built up.

In 1983-84 SCHA had 512 applications for housing, 134 from single women, 272 from single men, 41 from childless couples, 35 from two-parent families, and 30 from single-parent families. Of these 49 single women were housed, 153 single men, 18 childless couples, 11 two-parent families and 11 single-parent families, approximately half of those applying.

The cost per week of housing each successful applicant can be estimated (on the basis of annual income and number of people housed) at about £6 per person, or £24 per week per four-person family. Compared to the sums that councils pay for bed-and-breakfast accommodation for homeless familes – in 1976, for example, London boroughs were paying £59 per family per week; in 1984 Camden council was paying £280 per week for the housing of a family – it represents remarkably good value, even allowing for the difference that being in London makes.

In spite of the obvious advantages of self-help and short-life housing, SCHA has been set up, developed and continues to operate without any significant government support, spurred on solely by the commitment of its members and staff to providing suitable short-term and permanent accommodation for a growing number of homeless people. Without media 'hype' and without royal patronage, SCHA has helped thousands of homeless people in Bristol to house themselves.

Summary

The present case history is useful because it allows us to see the evolution of a popular housing organisation from unstructured informal squatting group to structured formal housing association, and to gauge what has been gained and lost along the way. This process has brought with it changes in attitudes, methods and structures at every level of activity, producing a very different organisation from that which existed initially. The main consequences of this transformation have been: a marked improvement in housing conditions for tenants and a corresponding reduction in their control of the process.

Starting as an illegal squatting group, SCHA had only available to it the wasted resources of modern society: empty houses, discarded building materials and the spare labour of its (mainly unemployed) members. The origin of formal activity was the need to end the wasteful, chronic conflict with owners and authorities, and to release the energies tied up in this conflict for more practical purposes (like repairing houses). Also, there was the possibility of access to official resources (like empty council properties and subsidy) as a result of current housing legislation. By becoming a housing association and obtaining legal use of properties, the group became a 'collective landlord'. This was the first step to formalising its activities, gradually coming to rely on rent capital to develop its operations, rather than on voluntary self-help by individual members.

The contractual needs of its landlord role (management and maintenance of properties) and the need to maintain a steady turnover of properties to remain viable in its development and maintenance functions, demanded an increasing professionalisation and forced a corresponding transformation at every level of operation.

At an organisational level, unstructured control by open meetings was discarded in favour of a more bureaucratic management committee model, borrowed from conventional housing associations. This change reduced participation by occupiers, which was already declining at other levels due to professionalisation. As participation decreased the management committee became a figurehead, and the main influence within the association became the 'collective' of paid staff, who now carried out all housing functions. From user-control the group passed to worker-control, with users being relegated to the role of 'consulted clients'.

Finances were also transformed, and informal reliance on members' good-will and their ability to carry out repairs became an increasing dependence on rental income and subsidy, particularly in view of the need for paid staff. Payment of rent became obligatory, and could be enforced by law. Contacts with the housing movement and local government allowed rent income to be supplemented with donations and subsidy, and initial repairs to be carried out with Housing Corporation funding. This progress demanded an even greater degree of financial control, to keep rent arrears down, maintain financial records and regularise employment practices.

At a technical level a corresponding evolution took place. From repairs being carried out by individual occupiers, this role was gradually assumed by semi-skilled workers, who gradually became part of the organising core of the association. The possibility of encouraging members to do their own repairs was discarded, since it seemed easier, more efficient, safer and probably cheaper (given the cost of training the occupiers) for staff to do the work. Only the curtailing of Urban Aid funding delayed SCHA from creating its own direct labour organisation. Development in this direction was also consistent with the group's Labour and trade union support. Since SCHA carried out both initial repairs and ongoing maintenance, it could guarantee that its building team continued in regular employment.

At the administrative level, SCHA staffing grew consistently over the years, and gradually differentiated functions. Eventually hierarchies were discarded, and all employees became 'workers' (development worker, finance worker, etc.) making decisions on a more collective basis.

There was a corresponding political shift. The squatting group's initial aims were fairly utopian and abstractly political ('expropriation of empty houses', 'housing for all', etc.), but real participation by the group and its members in local mainstream (not fringe) politics was minimal. As the association developed, links were forged with the Labour and trade union movement, and with the city's growing network of community organisations. These links were more practical than ideological, usually relating to the housing activities of the group. Growing influence in these quarters allowed more access to official resources, such as empty council houses and subsidy.

In conclusion, the passage from informality to formality transformed SCHA from an unstructured group of users housing themselves, to a structured group of professionals providing accommodation for homeless people, with little participation from them. This development was positive in some ways: thousands of families who would otherwise have been homeless or in inadequate bed-and-breakfast accommodation were housed, hundreds of empty properties which would have found no other use were repaired, housing conditions for occupiers were improved, and employment was created for a number of committed people which allowed their energy to be put to socially useful aims.

But something was also lost, that initial involvement and control over the housing process that ordinary people had acquired through the association in its early days. The temporary nature of the housing provided was partly to blame, since houses and occupiers pass very quickly through the organisation, not giving much time in which to develop real involvement. This involvement would be far more appropriate if the association provided permanent housing and members could have a say in design, participate in building, and manage the properties. This option has been closed to SCHA mainly because of its 'illegitimate' origins.

It is also likely that SCHA has not yet explored the possibilities of participation within its present legal structure, but has been prepared to discard it, along with the other utopian principles of its squatting days. As a substitute for its early unstructured participatory methods, SCHA has substituted the structured non-participatory ones of conventional housing associations and local authorities.

An alternative would be to try to actively develop participation at various levels of operation, for instance by promoting a structure for tenant management, by training occupiers to carry out building work, by providing more financial information so that members can have a say in what the rent is spent on. It could encourage an open forum for broader consultation, like the old weekly meetings, where homeless people could become involved in helping to house themselves.

5 | Self-build in Lewisham

The growth of Victorian London was probably similar to that of any major capital in the Third World today. Lord Rosebery, first chairman of London County Council, in 1881 described it as:

A tumour, an elephantiasis sucking into its gorged system half the life and blood of the rural districts.

The city's population grew by leaps and bounds. In 1800 there were 1 million inhabitants; by 1881, 4.5 million inhabitants; in 1911 this had increased to 7 million inhabitants. From 1800 to 1850 London doubled its physical size, and by the end of the century it spanned 18 miles across, from Edmonton to Croydon.

Although new industries created important sources of employment for the rural migrants, a large proportion was employed as domestic servants or in the 'service trades'. Unemployment swelled and shrank according to the whims of investment. A government survey of 1887 revealed 70 per cent unemployment among the working population. A further survey in 1892 showed that 30 per cent of the city's population lived in abject poverty. Housing conditions were predictably bad, with houses built near open sewers, badly constructed and without ventilation. The chronic risk of epidemic was increased by desperate overcrowding, fuelled by people's determination to be 'near their bread', or possible source of employment.

Clearance powers enabled the London County Council and the Metropolitan Board of Works to demolish whole areas, for 'sanitary' reasons, and to make way for railway or commercial developments. Five thousand had to move as land was cleared to build New Oxford Street. Communities living round stations, markets and docks were gradually thinned out. The inhabitants of these areas, already defeated by poverty and cowed by their

46

landlords, did little to fight these moves. Some were rehoused into properties provided by local authorities; most went on to overcrowd other slums. By 1911, nearly half of London's one-room tenements were recorded as overcrowded. At the same time the city's population was increasing by about 85,000 persons per year.

Several short-term solutions were proposed. One was the Cheap Train Act of 1883, which allowed Londoners to live in the cheaper outskirts of the city, and commute daily into work. This move was relatively successful, and over 300,000 rail fares per day were sold in 1902, rising to over 800,000 in 1913. This policy had the effect of expanding the suburbs, and accelerated the partition of the city on class lines, a division which has persisted to this day. Wealthier residents moved to the west and the higher ground of the north and south of the city. Working folk, rural migrants and immigrants swelled the east, south and north-east of the city.

A more fundamental solution was pioneered by the London County Council: the provision of municipal housing for workers. Using the powers given to them by the 1890 Housing Act, the council and the local boroughs had built, by the First World War, 3,883 and 1,682 dwellings respectively, in addition to 6,407 provided for rehousing. With Britain's entry into the war, further steps were taken towards state regulation and provision of housing. In 1915 rent controls were introduced, and 11,000 homes were provided directly by the Admiralty and the War Office from 1914 to 1918. The ground was paved for the development of mass municipal housing, as has been outlined in Chapter 3.

London's council housing

The Second World War had a devastating effect on Britain's housing. Much housing before the war was already obsolete and four million houses were already over 80 years of age. German air raids damaged one out of every three homes, totally destroying half a million.

As a response to these conditions, the post-war Labour government launched a Plan to 'relieve congestion and overcrowding in inner London and improve housing and living conditions for its communities'. The Abercrombie Plan proposed a ring of self-contained new towns outside London to house one million people from the inner city areas. Under this Plan, New Towns like Harlow, Basildon, Bracknell, Hemel Hempstead and Crawley, were built.

The London County Council and then the Greater London Council established many more 'expanded towns' such as Aylesbury, Bletchley, Banbury, Swindon, Andover, Basingstoke and Ashford.

Those left behind in the decaying inner cities were promised new housing, on modern estates made up of large systems-built blocks of flats, and a range of community facilities. But much of the housing built proved less than adequate, with few facilities, bleak design, poor maintenance. A community can hardly exist without the basic services and amenities – like shops, schools, meeting places and medical facilities – but these were often absent.

After the 1950s, subsidies were removed, and the need to compete for land on the open market eroded the possibilities of major council house building in inner London. New migrants to the city were particularly affected, almost inevitably ending up in slums. In one such area, Spitalfields, a 1981 survey found that 90 per cent of households living in overcrowded conditions were Bengali, and more than one in three families lacked basic amenities like a toilet, a bath or hot running water.

Post-war plans also encouraged, then did nothing to discourage, the running down of local jobs in central London. The removal of wholesale markets, the closure of the docks and the undermining of local industry by land speculation ruined the local economies on which community life depended. Asset stripping – the buying out of declining industrial companies to get their land and property holdings – became a source of easy profit. The land where housing and industries had once stood was now a much desired asset for the speculative office building. Because of this, in the mid-1960s, the Labour government imposed a ban on such developments in central London. This had the effect of giving speculators windfall prices for existing office space – rents went up from £5 per square foot in 1967 to £20 in 1973 – but availability of housing was decreasing. Richard Edmonds, Chairman of the LCC's Town Planning Committee stated in 1960:

To be successful the council's policy of restraint on further office growth in central London must be coupled with a policy of encouraging more homes to be built at the centre. If London is to retain its character as a living city by day, by night, it is essential to maintain a proper level of residential population in the heart of the capital.

'Homes Not Offices' became a public demand following the occupation of Centre Point – a large office block left empty in the heart of London by property speculator Harry Hyams, but, in fact, no effective action was taken against speculation.

Lewisham and the search for an alternative

Lewisham in 1970 contained many of the characteristics described above. Council housing accounted for 28 per cent of its housing stock, 32 per cent more being owner-occupied and the rest privately rented. Both private rental and private house building were in decline. At the end of the year Lewisham council had 2,119 dwellings under construction, in contrast to only 355 being built by the private sector. It would not be overstating the case to say that council housing was the fundamental source of housing for low-income people in Lewisham.

Lewisham's waiting list at the time was about 14,000 families long, and about 150 families were being accepted per year into 'temporary accommodation' as homeless persons. Of these roughly two-thirds were eventually rehoused into permanent housing, accounting for about 30 per cent of tenancies every year. The remaining 200-plus houses were allocated to persons at the top of the council's growing waiting list.

Until this time there is no record of a local authority promoting a self-build scheme directly, though self-build had been a fringe activity in the private sector for years, where it had been encouraged by specialist private consultants and some building societies. But these conventional self-build enterprises were not much different from commercial building operations. Self-build was usually carried out by small groups, often persons working in building, who wanted to use their 'spare labour' to provide themselves with a quality of home they could not otherwise afford. House designs and building technologies were often conventional, in order to meet the requirements of the building societies that funded the schemes. To achieve these conventional standards, self-building was usually organised along fairly rigid lines, where users were often little more than unpaid labourers, and skills had often to be bought in. Self-build was encouraged by the Housing Corporation, along similarly orthodox lines. It is not surprising, then, that such self-building has traditionally been viewed by local authorities as a 'private sector' activity.

Lewisham Self-Build

Like many pioneering breakthroughs, the Lewisham self-build project began as a lucky coincidence. Walter Segal, a Swiss architect with a private practice in London, had for some time been experimenting in the development of a low-cost timber-frame system, based on the American 'balloon frame'. Segal, a maverick breakaway from the Modern Movement, believed that the future lay in lightweight construction, rather than the heavy building techniques preferred by the mainstream movement.

The first dwelling built with his method was his own, a temporary structure while his permanent home was being rebuilt. This house (which is still standing today) was an assembly of easily available timber beams, infilled with common light-weight materials. It needed no foundations, standing on concrete slabs. It also sported an unusual flat roof, which instead of draining dry was designed to hold a layer of water. Segal's discovery was that this would protect the waterproof membrane from excessive thermal movement, thus avoiding cracks and leaks.

The house illustrated Segal's enlightened approach to building. Colin Ward, in his book *When We Build Again*, quotes him as saying:

> As I see it, buildings are there to be a background for people, against which they move, a background which envelops them, protects them, gives them pleasure, and allows them to add a little bit of themselves.

This initial building resulted in a series of private commissions, which Segal carried out in the UK and Ireland, with the help of a plumber, an electrician and a carpenter. The turning point came in 1971, when a teacher commissioned Segal to design and build his home in Suffolk. Having seen the carpenter begin to build the sparse timber structure, the teacher decided it would be cheaper to build it himself. He sacked the carpenter and went on to demonstrate the self-build possibilities of the Segal system.

By 1975, 25 dwellings of this type had been built, and Segal was interested in seeing the system applied to low-income housing. He then met Brian Richardson, assistant borough architect for Lewisham council. Richardson was also struck by its possibilities, which he saw as a potential alternative to the 'usual expensive council procedures'.

He presented the idea to Planning Committee chairman Nicholas Taylor, who suggested a report to the Housing Committee. Fortunately for all, the ruling Labour Group held an unusual view of 'municipal socialism'. For an article by Charlotte Ellis in *Architects' Journal*, Nick Taylor called it:

> Lewisham's libertarian vision of a socialism which is neither of the managerial Right nor the authoritarian Left, but which uses state intervention to release the creative energies of ordinary people.

In 1971, the Group accepted a report, drawn up by Councillors Taylor, Pepper and Broome, suggesting a return to the Garden City ideals of early council housing. It emphasised the need for individuality in housing provision. This fitted in well with the self-build proposal. In *Architects' Journal*, Charlotte Ellis again quotes Nick Taylor:

> What Walter has done is simply to update half-timber . . . The essence of what has been achieved here is real vernacular – not a cosmetic vernacular of gables and leaded lights, but a vernacular in the true sense, of ordinary people building with ordinary people's skills.

Richardson's report went to the Housing Committee in 1975 and was referred back for more information. In March 1976 the Committee reconsidered the proposal and approved it by a single vote. This approval authorised the selection of a group from the council's waiting and transfer list, the appointment of an architect, and the selection of sites from the council's difficult-to-use land bank.

Four sites were initially selected: a sloping clay hillside at Forest Hill; two pieces of scrubland in Sydenham; and a suburban garden on the Bromley border.

Selecting self-builders was the next step. An item in the council free newspaper *Outlook* asked people on the housing transfer and waiting list to write in for more details. Applicants were then invited to attend a public meeting with Walter Segal and council officers. One hundred and sixty eight people turned up, and the project was explained. Various proposals for the organising of groups were made, and a questionnaire was circulated to those attending. Finally, a voluntary Steering Group was selected, to work out the details of the project. The Steering Group later suggested the following principles:

– Applicants should be able to join, irrespective of age or income.
– The scheme should be open to all, irrespective of building skills.
– No capital should be required from self-builders.
– Each builder should be responsible for his own home, co-operating only on common tasks like main drains, fencing, paths, etc.
– There should be a guaranteed council mortgage for self-builders wanting to buy their own houses on completion.
– Finance should be on some sort of 'equity sharing' basis, where ownership would partly rest with the occupiers, partly with the council.

Many families were put off by the details of the project. Only 78 turned up at a second meeting, where the Steering Group proposals were accepted. Since only four sites had by then been selected, the number of families in the first stage was set at 14, and selected by ballot. The rest of the families were placed on a waiting list, in preparation for further projects.

Then the delays began. The DoE had no precedent for funding such schemes, so a funding system had to be devised, which included items like a 'notional allowance' which put a figure on the self-builders' labour contribution. Although the timber-frame system was designed in accordance with national building regulations, it did not comply with local building by-laws. Eventually, plans had to be amended, budgets changed and subsidies renegotiated.

Another hold-up was planning permission, which took five months. The worries of neighbours about the 'prefabs' being built next door were only set at rest by the production of attractive perspectives by the assistant borough architect.

Throughout this time, members of the groups went to evening classes especially set up for them, covering mainly measuring, cutting and drilling. The simple, modular basis of the construction system was explained to the families, and they were asked to draw their ideal houses on graph paper using those principles. The drawings were then analysed by Walter Segal, who discussed the options and possibilities with each family. Meetings were held to plan the eventual works, and plots were allocated.

By now the group had been waiting nearly three years since the first public meeting. Colin Ward records that Segal recalled:

> In the end even the council thought it was expecting too much and it was mainly Ron Pepper who said he would take it upon himself to let them go and clear the site; and later he authorised the first two houses to be done.

When this happened, Brian Richardson remembers that 'they hurled themselves to work faster than the materials could be supplied'.

Self-organisation

At the council's suggestion, the group registered as a self-build housing association with the Registrar of Friendly Societies, and affiliated to the National Federation of Housing Associations. But it put one rule from the Model Rules under which it registered into practice: the payment of £1 per week per family into communal funds. The rest, dealing with formal meetings, timetables and fines for non-attendance, were disregarded.

The final membership of the scheme was very diverse, ranging in age from 20 to 60. Since whole families participated, the participating age range was even wider. When the time came, every member of the family was welcome on the building site, including children. There were no rules or work parties; each family merely got on with the job of building its own house, and obtained materials and advice as required.

Every type of job was undertaken on a self-help basis, drainage, electrical and plumbing installations included. But this was not a rule – families could use the funds earmarked for a particular job to employ a contractor rather than doing the work themselves, though in fact none of them chose to do this. The one exception was roofing, where Segal insisted that a contractor be called in, to ensure the buildings were watertight.

The whole basis of the scheme was voluntary co-operation, with each family being ultimately responsible for building its own home. Nevertheless there was no difficulty in getting members to cooperate in the digging of drains, the erection of structural frames, or the moving and stacking of deliveries of heavy materials. On the whole, the approach was a success, and a feeling of community was developed. Colin Ward quotes one of the members:

> A wife had a baby the other week. The buntings were out and the balloons . . . If someone requires a babysitter, if someone is working on a car . . . or the communal garden . . . they get help. No-one tells them to do that, they do it themselves because they have control over where they are living and they contribute.

Members were also willing to work on each other's houses, if for some pressing reason the future occupiers were unable to work themselves.

Looking back on it, the self-builders reckon that stricter rules would have resulted in 'many members being thrown out on their ear, or with their marriages around their necks'. They also confirm that self-builders using this method do not need any particular building skills, and that any group with stamina and the support of their local authority is in a position to undertake such a project. But they disagree with Segal's original estimate of three months' total construction time. They think twelve months would be more accurate.

Architectural enabling

The architects considered detailed architectural drawings unnecessary for this type of project. Each self-builder was supplied with basic freehand plans and sections and a typewritten specification nine pages long, describing the sequence of construction. These were supplemented by site instructions, including construction sketches. The drawings gave only overall dimensions, so timber lengths had to be worked out by individual self-builders.

The idea behind this 'omission' was to encourage self-builders to work out dimensions themselves, and to understand plans thoroughly before starting to build. This seemed to work, and builders seem to have experienced difficulty only in interpreting staircase drawings. Other self-builders have suggested that three-dimensional drawings, or a step-by-step manual, would have been useful.

Certain modifications of the original design were necessary to obtain approval under London construction by-laws, but on the whole they seem rather trifling. One was that ceiling height had to be measured from the floor to the bottom end of the ceiling beam, rather than to the ceiling panel, which resulted in an extra 15cm having to be added to the overall height of the room. This change required complicated recalculations which delayed the scheme. The other was that pebbles, or concrete panels, would have to be laid under the whole extent of the ground floor under the houses. The purpose of this is not clear, but was perhaps connected with discouraging the residents from the 'keeping of pigs and rabbits', as a GLC official had warned they might do . . .

Building

Looking for contractors to carry out drainage excavations on the Forest Hill site, the council found all tenders to be over DoE cost-limits. The only option, therefore, was for self-builders to undertake the work themselves. They began digging under the supervision of the one member who had some drainage experience, hiring a JCB for one day.

The digging was more problematic than they had reckoned, due to waterlogging and old foundations under the surface. They succeeded in digging the whole trench (which was ten feet deep at one end) but omitted to put in enough shoring to support the trench walls. After a night of rains, the trench collapsed, and the JCB had to be recalled to do the job again. This time they propped the walls with jacks as they went along, and the trench held.

Foundations were usually no problem, since the single pier structure rested on concrete pads two feet square and (usually) three feet in depth. But on the Sydenham site a layer of made-up ground was found, and the families were asked to sink their pads to a depth of ten feet. This they did, painstakingly, by hand. Elsewhere on the same site a natural spring was found, which quickly filled the holes with water. Problems arose when holes had to be left open for the Building Inspector to approve, since the water eventually caved them in. Holes would then need disproportionate amounts of cement to fill.

One positive aspect of the pier system was that trees could be left to grow quite near the houses without affecting the foundations. Only if there was any danger of roots growing under concrete pads would these foundations have to be sunk deeper.

The carpentry required was basic, mainly sawing and drilling, without any complicated joins. The only important feature was ensuring that measurements (particularly of angles) were as accurate as possible. It was essential that the main frame be square and true in both horizontal and perpendicular directions.

The rest was simple. After the main frames had been built and raised, they were tied with beams and joists. The roof was covered with woodwool slabs, felted and the verges capped. Services could then be laid under the house, and the flooring put down. Services were then installed, and a 'sandwich' of asbestos-cement, woodwool and plasterboard used to infill the sections created by the timber frame. The 'sandwich' was then clamped together with bolted battens. The roofing operation was critical. Segal insisted that woodwool slabs should be laid down and roofs felted and pebbles put down on the same day. Since slabs had to be laid by self-builders before contractors could lay the felt, this caused quite a rush on the day. Worse, if the materials were not delivered or felters did not arrive, slabs could blow off, and the felt get damaged. Fortunately, this rarely happened. Pebbles were carried up in buckets by hand or using rudimentary pulleys. The amount of pebbles had to be carefully estimated so as not to over-stress the ceiling beams.

Once roofs had been laid, the rest was up to each family's energy and ingenuity. Although the general layout had been previously agreed, there was still opportunity for last-minute variations in kitchen layouts, fittings and types of doors. Such changes were common, as families learned from each other's ideas. The only minor detail which some members were not happy with was the use of the main bolts, which held the frame together and which showed on the inside of the walls.

Apparently it was easy for self-builders to follow the various specifications provided, both for the structure and for the installations. At first the local Building Inspector looked at work meticulously, to check that beams were not notched, pipes were lagged, etc. Later, when it became evident that the self-builders knew what they were doing, this supervision became less rigorous.

Supervision of works by Walter Segal and his colleague Jon Broome was, by all accounts, cordial and supportive. There was no question of careless work, since everyone was working on their own home. Regular site visits made it possible to discuss problems and suggest modifications. The self-builders say that the architects would usually persuade them to follow their advice, but several modifications, particularly to the choice of fittings and doors, were suggested by residents.

Forward planning was essential. as a self-builder stressed:

> You need to think at least three weeks ahead of what you're actually doing and get your materials on site when you need them. And you need to work out what you are going to do on site when you get there.

Purchase of materials had to be done through the council, and this proved rather complicated. The process was as follows: the architects produced drawings from which the quantity surveyors would draw up a schedule of materials. Self-builders ordered from this schedule as required, but only from approved suppliers. Suppliers then sent the invoices back to the Borough Architect, and a copy to the surveyors to check against the original schedule. When these were returned, certified as correct, the Borough Architect would order the Borough Treasurer to make the payment. The quantity surveyor would thus have a record of all the materials spent against the schedule, and ensure against possible overspending.

The situation became complicated, however, when a member changed a design detail and required different materials – the group felt that if purchasing had been left up to them, they could have used funds more flexibly and for better value. They were also unhappy with the fact that although overspending was not allowed, there was nothing to be gained by making savings.

The only electrical tools purchased by the group, from communal funds, were a circular saw and a drill for every three houses. Heavier plant was hired as required, and smaller tools provided by each member. The group felt it would have been useful to purchase more plant initially, if funds had been available at the begining of the project.

It is worth noting that the houses today remain in perfect condition. This is partly due to the nature of the technology, that facilitates maintenance, and of the detailed knowledge that each occupier has of his own dwelling. They have also proved easy to

extend and modify. One of the self-builders began extending his
dining area almost as soon as he moved in. Several other extensions
and additions have taken place – of bedrooms, for example, and
bay windows – as well as a general swapping round of features.

Tenure

In order to allow the council to make use of loan sanctions, and
for DoE subsidy to be applied, the houses were built as council
houses, and the self-builders, in effect, 'contracted' to build them
under a modified standard building contract. On completion of the
works they were each granted a 99-year lease, and the council
undertook to grant a mortgage on 50 per cent of the final valuation
of the property, less a nominal pre-payment equivalent to the
'notional value' of the self-builders' labour. The other 50 per cent
remains in council ownership, and the self-builders pay the
equivalent of 50 per cent of a current council rent. Self-builders
have the option to buy the rest of the property, in 10 per cent
instalments, from the council, until they own the whole property.

One curious detail of this project is that although most self-
building is tax-free, the Lewisham group has been taxed on the
notional payments credited to them for their labour. In a later
scheme this ruling was changed and the first self-builders are
currently trying to reclaim the tax.

After-effects

The success of the first Lewisham Self-Build scheme did not make
either the building system or the principles on which it was based
as popular with local authorities as expected. However, in 1984
a second Lewisham Self-Build project was launched, completed
in 1986.

Lewisham Self-Build II improved on the first scheme both in
terms of organisation and design. Rather than several houses
spread out through the borough, the second project involved the
construction of 13 houses on a sloping site in Honor Oak Park.
These houses were bigger than those of the first scheme: 79-83
square metres of floor space. And this time 19 variants were offered
to self-builders, with a range of optional modifications.

Conventional self-build, if not the Walter Segal method, at any
rate has become popular with the private sector. *The Observer*

noted that during 1986 there were over 13,000 self-build starts. These were mainly 'youngsters wanting to own larger homes for less money, or to get quickly on the housing ladder, missing out some of the bottom rungs as they do so'. The building methods and materials used are conventional, and the funding comes from building societies.

Local authorities have not been oblivious to this trend. Stirling Council has appointed Rod Hackney & Associates to design and co-ordinate a self-build and self-repair scheme in Colquhoun Street. Other councils throughout the country have embarked on similar projects.

The Housing Corporation has also been willing to support some innovative self-build projects: an overdraft guarantee from them allowed the Zenzele Self-Build Housing Association in Bristol (made up of a dozen young people, mainly black and unemployed) to build their own homes.

But these examples are unusual. On the whole, self-build has not been integrated as a form of local authority or housing association provision. It remains the domain of the private sector, fostered by private consultants who charge an average of 10 per cent of the cost of works, exclusive of architectural fees. For this reason perhaps it remains a sort of mirror image of the conventional, commercial building process, and out of bounds to most people on low incomes.

Summary

The present case history demonstrates how, even in a developed society, a local housing authority can fund and promote a successful self-build project as an alternative or complement to its normal provision. Given the availability of adequate professional support and appropriate technologies and organisational models, the results can be cheaper and better than contracted options.

Finance for this scheme came entirely from the local council, through its Housing Revenue Account (which is supported from rates and a central government grant), and from individual low-interest mortgages to occupiers. This arrangement involved less subsidy than is made available for the building of council housing, but standards were higher. This was thanks to a reduction in building costs, through self-help, and to the use of an appropriate building system.

The building land comprised 'hard to use' plots owned by the council. These plots could not have been developed within cost-limits for conventional new building. Through the use of the Segal technology, building costs were lower than conventional building on less problematic sites. Failing this use, these plots would probably have remained vacant, or been sold at reduced rates.

Some drains were dug directly by the self-builders, although responsibility for the provision of external services and infrastructure remained with the council and the service boards, and was carried out without problems. Considerable delay did arise, however, from having to meet apparently unnecessary technical and administrative requirements, both in terms of planning regulations and funding arrangements.

Initiative for the scheme came from the council, who formed the community through a public meeting of people on their waiting and transfer list. Those who chose to pursue the project were brought together into an autonomous self-build housing association, and were able to control, within limits, the design of the houses, the organisation of work, and the priorities given to the funding available. Self-help works on the project were organised on what might be called a 'libertarian' model (known as Building Together Apart), which allows maximum freedom to each self-builder (in this case individual families) within an overall plan under the supervision of the project architects.

The strict rules and regulations of conventional self-build were thus avoided, likewise any complicated 'collective' work organisation which would place additional obligations on individual members. This was mainly thanks to the pre-industrial nature of the building system used, which did not require a stratified labour organisation. Individual familes were free, within the limits of the overall programme, to work how they wanted and when they wanted, and there was no dependence on others in the building of individual houses. The only exception was work on communal facilities (like drains) which were carried out on the basis of voluntary co-operation. This method of working reduced potential conflicts and created a feeling of independence and solidarity among members. It certainly contributed to the creation of a community among residents.

Participation extended to the design of the houses, and individual work programmes and supply schedules were the responsibility of each self-builder, in consultation with the project architects. Self-builders could, if they wished, modify the building procedures suggested and the construction details, within limits.

Overall financial administration of the project was in the hands of the council, and this created some difficulties in co-ordination, particularly in the buying of materials. The funding arrangement might have been more effective if the association could have worked to a fixed budget, while being ultimately accountable to the council.

The architects performed an 'enabling' role throughout the project, and at no point attempted to take over the running of the group. Rather than dispensing professional truths, they advised and encouraged the self-builders to put their own ideas into practice. They developed a simple 'construction language', which they encouraged the self-builders to learn and use. This relationship gave users a high degree of confidence and control over construction, only limited by the technical and financial constraints of the project. These limits became a sort of frame within which the self-builders worked, rather than ready-made criteria to be absorbed uncritically.

The building technology was a vital asset to the group, and without it things would probably have had to be organised differently. Some of its obvious advantages were:
– It used cheap materials available locally.
– The materials used did not require much work done on them before they were assembled, and assembly was simple.
– The structural principles of the building were easy to understand, and could be modified according to preference.
– Construction could be carried out by relatively unskilled people.
– Few expensive tools were needed.
– House types were culturally acceptable – 'updated vernacular'.

The building system, and the corresponding methods of organising construction, were appropriate to the scale, possibilities and preferences of the user-group. The housing produced was therefore much more tailored to the individual families concerned than the equivalent municipal provision would have been. They were also far more flexible than conventional housing, so could be modified and repaired with ease. For these reasons, user-satisfaction has been high, and problems are very unlikely to arise

	Bromley 1 single-storey 1 two-storey	Sydenham 1 single-storey 2 two-storey	Sydenham 2 two-storey	Forest Hill 7 single-storey
Materials and other payments	£9,335	£10,244	£11,030	£10,366
Labour allowance	£4,683	£5,056	£4,872	£5,769
Increased cost allowance	£2,190	£3,633	£3,768	£4,701
TOTAL	£16,208	£18,933	£19,670	£20,836
Total cost per person	£3,602	£3,787	£3,934	£4,167
Cost per m² of gross floor area	£218/m²	£230/m²	£224/m²	£251/m²

– The Forest Hill site had higher costs because of the characteristics of the site, in spite of drainage work being done on a self-build basis. This was because of large roofing area that had to be covered by contract work.

– In the Sydenham site, cost of materials for external perimeter details was high.

– 60% of the works carried out were 'conventional' building operations, but the building system used allowed a high self-build input which reduced overall cost.

– The pier system, eliminating expensive foundations (especially on tricky ground) kept cost to a minimum.

– Some bulk buying and storage allowed reduction of further costs due to inflation.

Costs of Lewisham Self-Build.

from lack of maintenance, vandalism or associated management problems.

This project and the systems employed were appropriate to Lewisham, but could not necessarily be applied anywhere else without modification. In particular, it has not been demonstrated that this method would be appropriate for larger projects, where more co-ordination and the creation of a larger community was required.

There is little doubt however that the project brought many direct benefits to the people concerned, apart from good quality housing and the creation of a community. But since the initiative depended on the goodwill and financial support of the council, the possibilities of repeating the scheme outside Lewisham are limited unless other authorities show the same degree of support. To date no other local authority has shown that, although in Brighton the council is apparently considering a scheme and the Housing Corporation showing some interest in the system. Although this indicates a thaw, it is still a long way to acceptance of the Segal system as a viable way for people housing themselves.

6 | Participatory design in Liverpool

Liverpool is one of England's legendary sea-ports about which much has been written and sung. Daniel Defoe, in the early 1700s, called it 'one of the wonders of Britain'. During the 18th century, the population increased from 5,000 in 1700, to 34,407 in 1773. By 1768, its growth was entirely dependent on mercantile activity around the four main docks, so most buildings were within 1,000 yards of the river. By the end of the century the building of dwellings for the labouring classes was concentrated in the south and north of the city.

A common form of working class housing at this time was the 'cellar dwelling', examples of which still exist today. These were underground garrets, often under better-off residences, whose floors could be as much as six feet below ground level. They usually had no sanitary facilities, light or ventilation. They were also prone to flooding. Without alternatives at affordable rents, they provided the most common type of housing for workers of the day. A building surveyor described a typical scene:

> Sometime ago I visited a poor woman in distress, the wife of a labouring man; she had been confined only a few days, and herself and infant were lying on straw in a vault, through the outer cellar, with clay floor impervious to water. There was no light or ventilation in it, and the air was dreadful. I had to walk on bricks across the floor to reach her bedside, as the floor itself was flooded with stagnant water. This is by no means an extraordinary case. (*The History of Working-Class Housing*, J. H. Treble)

By 1841 nearly 34 per cent of the city's population lived in cellars like these, fanning the first sparks of municipal intervention in an effort to close them down.

Another form of low-income housing provision by the private sector were 'courthouses', or the hated 'back-to-backs' that are still being cleared today. These were designed with financial expediency and the maximisation of profits in mind, and with little regard for the conditions inflicted on occupiers. They usually consisted of:

> Two facing rows of houses, each row containing between two and eight dwellings. Such houses would normally be three storeys high, and consist of two rooms 10 or 11 feet square and a garret, though there might often be a cellar attached which . . . would inevitably be sublet. Externally the distance between each row could be a little as six feet.

These narrow courts were closed at the end by a high wall, so access to the houses was through a narrow passage. Backing onto each court would be another row of identical houses, until all available land was filled. In spite of predictable overcrowding and health problems due to bad ventilation, by 1840 25 per cent of the city's population lived in these warrens.

Building of dwellings like these went on in fits and starts, according to the income then currently available to working people to pay rent, and to the general availability of investment capital to local developers, who were, in the main, members of the legal profession. From 1800 to 1838 a boom in the building of low-income dwellings took place, but it was followed by a practical freeze on such building.

The housing shortage, with its associated problems, was then increased by the Irish Famine of 1840, which brought waves of starving, often disease-ridden Irish labourers and their families to the sea-port. Given the already insalubrious standard of housing available, it is not surprising that working-class areas became 'plague spots', where typhoid, cholera and tuberculosis were common, encouraged by the general lack of services and sanitary facilities. The average lifespan in Liverpool at this time was 26 years, and one out of every seven children died before the age of five.

Municipal intervention

In 1842 Liverpool Corporation secured powers allowing it to

intervene in the private sector in order to improve sanitary conditions. Under this Health Act courts were required to be at least 15 feet wide and paved, and drainage and minimum ventilation and sanitary facilities were to be provided, at the owner's expense. It also required the closing down of cellars that could not meet minimum requirements of floor depth, light and ventilation. The Corporation also undertook to provide neighbourhood baths and wash-houses, and the local waterworks was municipalised to make this possible.

These, and subsequent regulations, met with the determined opposition of the local financially interested parties, who said they could not build with these restrictions, and of the impoverished workers themselves, who were prepared to flout legislation in order to keep a roof over their heads. The Corporation would not be deterred, however, and by 1851 an estimated 5,000 cellars – occupied primarily by Irish immigrant families – had been closed. But since no rehousing was provided, they went on to swell already overcrowded neighbouring areas.

Housing by co-operation, or the 'blood for blood' system, surfaced briefly around this time. It was primarily accessible to building tradesmen, who could request payment in land for services rendered to the gentry. Homes would then be 'self-built', with help from fellow tradesmen who would later expect equivalent services. These houses do not appear to have been noticeably different from others built at the time, probably because they were 'trade-based', using the same materials and techniques as conventional house building. This trend was never popularised, and was eclipsed by the advent of municipal housing.

In 1864 Liverpool Corporation obtained further powers, allowing it to demolish slums. By this time the Corporation already had wider powers than any local authority in England. Even so, the Act was not widely applied until 1884, when 1,000 houses were demolished. The number rose to 1,700 by 1890. To this must be added the demolition of many more houses (not all unfit) for development of transport and commerce, and the continuing closure of cellars. The pressure was great for some sort of housing to be provided directly by the Corporation.

In 1869 Liverpool built the first 124 Corporation cottages, to house families displaced by slum clearance. In 1885 a further 282 flats were built, and 102 more in 1891. Already a future trend in municipal housing was becoming evident: only a fraction of those in need were rehoused, and usually the poorest remained homeless. In 1890 the Housing of the Working Classes Act attempted to redress this injustice by making it the responsibility of the Corporation to rehouse at least 50 per cent of those made homeless by slum clearance. This helped to increase the rate of provision, and some building was undertaken on the outskirts of the city. But the rate of building did not match the rate of demolition, let alone take into account the growth of the city. Housing was primarily a private sector activity and municipal building only accounted for 9 per cent of the total.

By 1914, nearly 22,000 houses had either been demolished, closed or repaired for health reasons or to make way for development of transport and commerce. At the same time only 2,824 Corporation dwellings had been built, primarily in tenement blocks, but there were also some 'workers' cottages'. After the First World War, Liverpool was one of Britain's biggest cities, with a population of 817,000 and an estimated yearly deficit of 7,750 dwellings, on top of an unmeasured (but large) accumulated deficit. After the Addison Act of 1919, passed by the radical post-war government, which made the Corporation the city's biggest house builder, an estimated 5,808 houses were built. The municipal effort was, however, directed primarily at building in the suburbs, rather than demolishing the slums.

After a Conservative interlude, when subsidies were available to private builders but not the Corporation, the Wheatley Act (1924) was brought in, and a further 13,448 houses built for rental by the Corporation. From then until the Second World War municipal house building continued but was erratic, dependent on current politics and subsidies. If Labour was in power, subsidies would be increased and new building took place, usually in the suburbs. If Tories were in power, subsidies would be strictly limited to rehousing people from slum clearance, and building to inner-city blocks of flats made to low standards.

Although 22,192 dwellings were provided by Liverpool Corporation from 1919 to 1931, only 6 per cent were built directly by the council; the rest were built by private builders under contract. Private builders also provided, during this period, 4,294 subsidised dwellings for sale, and 3,292 unsubsidised.

The estates built soon after the First World War (and before subsidies were cut) were of relatively high standard, providing solid houses in Georgian style, grouped by blocks of four, about 12 to the acre. Space for shops, schools and churches (but not licensed premises) were also provided.

When the trend shifted towards slum clearance, walk-up tenement blocks in central areas of the city were favoured. This was consolidated with a reduction in subsidy for new housing in 1931, subsidy being only available per tenant rehoused. Ironically, reformers of the day saw the walk-ups as positive, collectivising influences. George Orwell described them as 'definitely fine buildings'.

Municipal building came to a standstill during the Second World War but swelled again as a result of the post-war Labour victory. Nationally, there was a brief return to the Garden City ideal of family houses with gardens in the suburbs. Liverpool, however, maintained a preference for walk-ups and high-rise flats that was to last until the 1970s.

In 1955 the Liverpool Labour Party secured control of the Corporation under the leadership of Jack and Bessie Braddock, two stalwart municipal socialists. They became, respectively, Leader and Deputy Leader of the Labour Group, as well as presiding over the Liverpool Trades Council. The Braddocks apparently promoted massive, centralised solutions to Liverpool's chronic housing shortage. This coincided with a time when Government and industry had begun a drive for more high-rise building and ever-rising densities, irrespective of tenants' preferences. The combination of centralised municipal socialism and high-tech 'systems building' had a devastating effect on the environment and its inhabitants, as Anne Grosskurth described in an article for the Shelter publication *Roof*:

> The Braddocks are today credited with the 'blitzkrieg' approach to redevelopment characteristic of Liverpool in that period. It was under their control that acres of terraced housing was knocked down, leaving a legacy of tower blocks and vacant sites.

Another of Liverpool Corporation's initiatives around this time was the construction of New Towns, the first of which was Kirby, as overspills for the city's population. The New Town was a 'maxi-estate' with commercial areas and other facilities. Kirby soon housed more than 60,000 people. It was followed up with other New Town projects, like Runcorn and Skelmersdale.

By 1966 Liverpool Corporation had become the main source of housing in the area, both inside and outside the city. Approximately 30 per cent of all local housing was rented out by the Corporation. The preference (on the Corporation's part) for high-rise accommodation continued. Of the units built between 1970 and 1975 50 per cent were one-bedroom flats; 29 per cent were two-bedroom flats; 17 per cent were three-bedroom houses; and only 4 per cent were four-bedroom houses.

Conditions in high-rise blocks were the target of increasing criticism: Lawrence Gardens, a walk-up block, was set in the middle of a ten-acre motorway loop and therefore completely cut off. Its demolition was proposed in 1966, and many flats boarded up. The decision was subsequently reversed, and by 1974 six flats were still occupied, amid widespread dereliction and vandalism. In a local Community Development Unit report, *Government Against Poverty?*, Topping and Smith described the buildings as: 'grilled, barred and draped in barbed wire, as if the area was dug in against assault from official and unofficial demolition.' Even pubs and shops were boarded up during the day in order to prevent damage. Not all the problems were technical: tightly knit communities had been broken up in the clearance and rehousing process, destroying the spirit of the neighbourhoods. This, combined with unresponsive council management and lack of maintenance, led to vandalism and violence.

When the building of high-rise blocks stopped, after 1972, the harm was already done. By 1982, roughly one-third of Liverpool's 75,000 council units were classified as 'hard to let'. Some 6,000 council homes were empty because no-one wanted to live in them, and many high-rise blocks were being demolished. There was even an instance, described by Nick Wates for the *Architects' Journal*, of 1950s walk-up blocks having their floors cut at single-storey level at the cost of £20 million. Although there were still homeless families, there was a theoretical housing 'surplus' made up of dwellings that no-one would live in.

This situation created an undercurrent of local discontent, which did not find expression in any of the traditional parties. It surfaced briefly in 1972, when the Campaign Against the Housing Finance Act (a Conservative Act that sought to raise council rents to Fair Rents level) succeeded in persuading 50 per cent of tenants in affected properties to withhold rents. The Labour Party, although officially opposed to the Act, did not support the Campaign. In 1973 tenants launched their own candidates against Labour candidates at local elections. They came second to Labour, showing the extent of disaffection with Labour's position. After this one show of strength, however, the tenants' movement practically disappeared, and in 1975 a new Labour government repealed the Housing Finance Act.

Co-operative housing

The recent co-operative housing movement in Liverpool first arose as a result of the Shelter Neighbourhood Action Project (SNAP), based in Granby Street, one of the city's General Improvement Areas. The initial aim of the Project was to prevent the fragmentation of communities during the process of slum clearance, and therefore it turned to co-operative housing. SNAP supported the setting up of the Granby Street Housing Co-operative, which used Corporation grants and mortgages to improve existing terraces. A second co-operative at Canning Street was set up with the aim of preserving one of Liverpool's stately Georgian squares and avenues. Together they formed the city's first secondary housing organisation, Neighbourhood Housing Services (NHS), to give advice to emerging co-ops.

With the 1974 Housing Act, which gave housing associations a more important role in public housing and increased the funding possibilities of the Housing Corporation, Liverpool adopted a strategy of housing association-based area renewal. This gave rehabilitation co-ops (those which preserved existing buildings) a boost, and eight more were formed in inner city areas.

In 1975, the London-based secondary co-operative, Co-operative Development Services (CDS), was invited to Liverpool to support the work of primary co-operatives. This experience led to the creation of a local offshoot, CDS (Liverpool), with local tenant representatives forming part of the managing corps. By 1977 housing co-operatives in Liverpool had rehabilitated more than 1,000 homes.

Public housing phase 2

By the end of 1977, CDS (Liverpool) was working with a group of 'clearance' families who had decided to build their own dwellings, under the name of the Weller Streets Housing Co-operative. The families, all of whom lived in dilapidated 'back to backs', set up a committee to pursue these objectives, chaired by a dynamic local milkman, Billy Floyd, who was able to galvanise members and keep them informed on a daily basis through his rounds.

The members of the Weller Streets co-op were real pioneers. They obtained £1.3 million of Housing Corporation money to buy land in their neighbourhood and build new homes, designed to their specifications, to be owned, controlled, managed and maintained by themselves. The possibilities of participation in designing new-build were much greater than those in rehabilitation, so co-op members for the first time had a chance to design their own homes.

Participatory design, a new architectural philosophy and practice, where users, rather than professionals, make the decisions was developed to make this arrangement operative. Since the co-op was being funded directly, they were relatively free to choose their architects and builders, ensuring that only 'enabling' professionals were selected for these roles. They also had a considerable amount of influence on their development agent, CDS, who had helped form the group; the architects were a Liverpool practice, Building Design Group. This was one of the first experiments with the techniques of participatory design – using simple sketches, models, audio-visual aids – which would later become popular with Liverpool co-ops.

In Weller Streets the design achieved was 'simple and utilitarian'. A standard brick finish was used throughout, 'frills' dispensed with, and a high standard of materials and insulation worked to. Landscaping was also given a high priority. Given the choice of managing and maintaining the properties themselves (as a co-op) or contracting this function to CDS, the members chose the former. The background to this decision is described in the book *The Weller Way* by Alan McDonald. The book is particularly interesting because it shows the constant struggle of the co-op not to lose control of their project to 'the professionals' – who they expected to be 'on tap but not on top'.

Weller Streets housed 61 families and was described by Nick Wates as:

The fastest housing association new-build scheme on

Merseyside, from land registration to start on site. So much for the argument that participation slows the process down too much.

Hesketh Street Housing Co-operative

Liverpool's second new-build housing co-operative came into being in February 1979. The co-op was a direct product of the municipal slum clearance programme, and was formed by tenants of a condemned terrace. They were later joined by a second group of council tenants who had lived in Hesketh Street before the terrace had been demolished by the Corporation, and who were looking for an opportunity to regroup and return. As luck would have it, both groups converged on CDS, who had some time before been offered the Hesketh Street site by the Corporation. The two groups – both composed of working-class families, with some unemployed and some old age pensioners – came together to form Hesketh Street Housing Co-operative.

The role of CDS was that of a guiding hand and professional development agency. There seems little evidence of the primary/ secondary conflict recorded in the Weller experience. CDS's main function throughout the scheme was to provide advice and education, and to carry out the administrative tasks involved in development (such as site purchase and briefing of architects). The role of this professional body was clearly spelled out from the start in a 'Co-operative Development Agreement', where the duties and responsibilities of each party were set out. This arrangement was important in that it limited the professional organisation's area of control, and gave the co-op a greater degree of self-determination.

The starting point of CDS's work with the group was to teach it the 'client role', so that it could make full use of the control offered by the arrangement. Housing Corporation funding available for 'co-operative education' was used to explain housing association finance to co-op members and to teach and develop administrative skills. A series of briefings were organised, to provide co-op members with the information to make decisions.

A primary topic was the selection of architects by the co-op. CDS explained the role of the architect, followed by detailed practice information from a shortlist of seven local architectural practices with private and public housing experience. On the basis of visits to finished projects, the shortlist was reduced to four, and after preparatory meetings, interviews were carried out and a final selection made.

Another of CDS's functions was to brief architects for the project, so they understood not only the particular requirements of Housing Corporation funding, but also the extent to which they would be expected to inform and educate the co-op in the design process.

Throughout the project, CDS maintained an 'unobstructive presence', ensuring that the co-op had information on which to base decisions; that project targets and deadlines were met; and that Housing Corporation requirements and procedures were being adhered to. CDS, as development agent, also negotiated site purchase, dealt with loan applications and grant submissions, rent registrations, and other financial procedures and statutory requirements, some of which were carried out jointly with the project architects.

A further CDS educational function was the preparation of co-op members for future management and maintenance of the estate. Training sessions were conveniently carried out during the construction stage of the project. Instruction was given on 'the responsibilities of being a collective landlord'. Tenancy agreements were discussed and drawn up, lettings policy and re-allocation policy (including giving the Corporation 50 per cent nomination rights) were agreed. The administrative and accountancy services for estate management were set up, and a service agreement drawn up between the co-op and CDS, outlining the various accounting and maintenance services that the latter would provide when the scheme was complete.

Funding

Capital funding was eventually provided by the Housing Corporation under the Housing Association Grant (HAG) arrangements set out in the 1974 Housing Act and DoE Circular 11/77. This legislative package provides for one-off capital subsidy (HAG) to approved association or co-operative schemes, to cover costs which cannot be met by a mortgage at commercial rates undertaken on the basis of rental income. HAG makes up the gap between the total cost of the scheme and what the association (or co-operative) can afford. At the same time, rents have to be set at Fair Rent level, and a proportion of rents have to be deducted for yearly management and maintenance, before the 'residual mortgage' can be estimated. Building costs, including architects' fees and administrative cost of development, are met on the basis of regular loan advances from the Housing Corporation. Current professional fee scales operate, and at the time of this project so did the Parker Morris Standard and cost-yardstick, which determined minimum spaces and quality of work, and at the same time limited the amount that could be spent on each item. They applied both to housing association and council building, and were considered both the floor and the ceiling of public housing expenditure.

As development agents, CDS dealt with the financial and legal transactions required for the project, including loan applications, purchase of land, contracting of design and construction, and liaison with architects, builders and the co-op. Cost of these activities were met from standard allowances within the HAG funding system. At the time the 'Co-operative Promotion Allowance' had not yet been introduced. Additional co-op education costs were met from a Section 121 grant of £15,000 per annum which CDS received from the Housing Corporation for its work with various local co-ops.

There is no doubt that many hidden costs were not met by any kind of funding, particularly in terms of extra time spent on the project by members, architects and CDS. These represent an unquantifiable voluntary contribution to the project.

Participatory design

The site chosen for the project was in an attractive part of the city, very different from the decaying slums of Liverpool. Working-class cottages had originally stood there, backing onto the grand houses of Livingstone Drive. This whole fringe of Sefton Park had been declared a Conservation Area in 1976. The area was served by modern shops, restaurants and wine bars, and was in every way an ideal site for a model co-op scheme.

From the final shortlist of possible architects, the co-op selected a local practice, Innes Wilkin, Ainsley, Gommon, to 'help' design the Hesketh Street scheme. David Innes Wilkin has given a detailed account of his experience as architectural consultant of the project for *Architects' Journal*: the selection took place after visits to examples of the architects' work and an interview lasting one hour, where these, and other, questions were put to him and his partner, Peter Gommon:

– Who will run the job in the practice, you or somebody else?

- What do you think of municipal housing?
- How will you educate us to help us make decisions?
- What is your ambition?
- How soon can we start on site?
- Can you afford to wait a long time (up to a year) for fees?
- What was the worst mistake you ever made as an architect?

After the architects had been selected, design could not begin until every member was equally informed as to the design possibilities available to them. The following steps were therefore taken:

- Coach trips and guided tours of about ten other housing schemes in the area (mainly in the Warrington and Runcorn developments) were organised.
- Slides were shown of the houses seen on these trips and other examples visited by the architects around the country.
- Books and magazines were circulated, showing selected housing layouts and details (e.g. *GLC-Preferred Dwellings, Space in the Home, Metric House Shells*).
- Overhead projection (at meetings) of coloured plans took place in order to add comments and extra items to them during discussion.
- A4 plans were circulated, as well as kits of small drawings and notes, for discussion and amendment at meetings. The site plan was also distributed on A2 sheets.
- Video film was taken on site and shown, with an explanation by the architects.
- Samples of material and landscape details were viewed at the practice office, the Brick Library in the Building Centre, and the University Botanical Gardens in Cheshire.
- Site models were constructed in polystyrene.
- A 'participation in house planning' model, loaned by Tony Gibson of Nottingham University was used, which forms rooms at 1:20 scale with card walls which can be moved around, and which include furniture, doors and windows.

In addition to these basics, members had to understand, and take into account, the following:

Use of space was limited by standards. Co-op members visited the DoE in Manchester and the Housing Corporation in Liverpool in order to discuss storage standards and provision for disabled members. They were advised of the required Parker Morris Standards.

Design was limited by cost-yardstick. The co-op met a quantity surveyor, who advised on density targets, and of design restrictions due to financial limits.

Planning restrictions. The Planning Office wrote a brief for study by the co-op, and neighbours and local firms asked to voice their suggestions and objections at meetings with the co-op.

Design variations. Requirements of certain members (through disability, for example, or large families) differed from the norm, and had to be separately considered.

Roads. After discussion, the co-op decided to comply with the Borough Engineer's requirements, and have roads 'adopted'.

Parking requirements. Regulations regarding minimum parking space were in force. However, a planning agreement was drawn up to reduce the normal requirement, since few co-op members had cars. It was agreed that garden space should be earmarked for extra parking space, should it be required in the future.

Organisation of design

A full meeting of more than 40 members proved an unwieldy forum in which to make design decisions, so a design committee was formed, made up of ten voluntary members (primarily women, who had more flexible timetables). This design committee met with the architects every week. It included any other members who could make it, and a representative from CDS. The meetings were held in somebody's flat, or in a local meeting room, and were strictly timed and minuted. Apart from these design meetings, individual surgeries were also held with each family, particularly at the beginning and the end of the design process. These surgeries included members of the design committee, who acted as mediators between the architects and individual members.

Minutes and recommendations of both the design meetings and the surgeries would be read out at the monthly general meetings, where members would be informed of decisions and asked to ratify them. Examples of points discussed at these meetings were the need for deeper kitchen units and the space allowed for tall fridge-freezers.

Once the precise mix of members was known, sketch proposals could begin. First came a density exercise, to check yardstick costs with the quantity surveyor, and to check the mix of household sizes with the Housing Department. Then a detailed survey of members' preferences was carried out. The design committee helped individual members to answer the questionnaires. Sketch proposals helped members to make detailed choices.

On the basis of the sketches and the survey, the following (and other) topics were discussed and determined:

Internal and external storage. The co-op decided against external stores and to have the required storage area internally.

Kitchen at front or rear. The co-op decided, with one exception, to have kitchens at the rear of the houses.

Dining area separate or in kitchen or living room. There was much variation, in contrast to upper rooms, which were similarly laid out.

Open or enclosed stairs. Most people wanted the living room to appear larger by omitting the hall partition.

Windows – size, method of opening, finish and security. Drawings showing the different options were presented, and the decision was for timber-framed hung casements.

Garden size. Few members had ever had gardens before, but different requirements were accommodated, thanks to the irregular shape of the site.

Choice of materials. Bricks and roof tiles, along with doors and kitchen units, were chosen after seeing samples.

Trees and landscaping. Many families were originally opposed to landscaping (which was considered 'Corpie', and associated with cutting-off municipal estates from surrounding housing).

Communal open spaces. These were generally disliked, because of the feeling they encouraged vandalism and maintenance problems. In the final scheme there was little communally maintained space, and grounds were the responsibility of houses that they fronted.

All these decisions were made on the basis of talks, slide shows and visits arranged by the architects and CDS. By the time the scheme was out to tender, 100 design meetings had taken place, all minuted.

During design, great pains were taken to ensure that every house fitted the site in the best possible way (e.g. by putting large houses needing a gable bathroom window at the end of the terrace). When the site and house plans were finalised, and the location of each house determined, the co-op committee decided that the houses could best be allocated by general agreement (rather than by lot, as other co-ops had done previously). This was achieved without too much trouble, and people continued to 'exchange' houses until everyone was satisfied.

The Hesketh Street Housing Co-operative development (officially known as Newlands Court) is made up of 40 households, divided into 16 flats, one of which was especially designed for a disabled person, and 24 houses: four two-person flats, 12 three-person flats, nine four-person houses, nine five-person houses, five six-person houses, and one seven-person house.

Construction

At the beginning of the design period, builders were asked to offer package deals (two-stage tenders) for the project. Employing this method would have limited the design input from the co-op, but members were interested in comparing speed of construction to traditional methods. Two-stage tenders were eventually dropped because contractors were not able to deal with desired design variations, and because the environmental and finished quality of the scheme would have been lower than what the co-op wanted. The co-op therefore invited traditional tenders from eight contractors, out of a short-list of 20, selected after examples of work had been visited.

The lowest tender exceeded the yardstick, so a number of amendments and deletions to the schedule of works had to be made. This was done at a meeting of the co-op that voted on a list of items to be eliminated or changed. The essence of the voting was to uphold the quality of basic elements, and leave out secondary items that could be improved or added later. The tender was accepted in January 1982, and work on site began three months later. But when a public drain was discovered on site, requiring the Corporation's intervention, the scheme was delayed a further 11 weeks.

Although co-op members visited the site while construction was under way, and were involved in site meetings by the contractor and his staff, all official site instructions were made through the architects, to avoid confusion.

Exteriors

Reports on the general appearance of the project consistently point out the balance, or harmony, achieved between aesthetic and functional qualities: in colours – between the polychrome brickwork and the landscaped grounds; in materials – between hard (brick and tile) and soft (grass and trees) landscape; in decorative versus functional details – apparently decorative extras like 'thrust' porches or garden walls are useful as well as attractive; in the individuality of each house versus the cohesiveness of the scheme as a whole – each house is tailored to its residents, but is very much part of the estate; between limited resources and maximum quality – the value of each item and detail has been weighed by residents with a view to limited resources and future maintenance.

Conventional architectural tricks aimed at easy savings (like putting storage space in flimsy sheds at the back of houses) were rejected by the co-op. Although the design of the exteriors was largely left up to the architects (as opposed to the interiors, where every decision was deliberated), this was only after co-op members had formed a clear idea (on the basis of visits to other projects and several discussions) of what the architects were likely to do. Nonetheless, observers have detected a certain 'architectural paternalism' in the exteriors, which is certainly not evident in the interiors.

One item that the architects had to argue for, however, was 'perimeter planting' around the grounds. Many co-op members were opposed to this, on the grounds mentioned above. After viewing more integrated examples of landscaping in nearby New Towns, the co-op accepted this suggestion.

Interiors

This is where the real individuality of Hesketh Street is evident, and where the attention of the families was focused. The principle of 'fixed shell and changeable scenery' was applied, allowing first-time occupants to organise the inside of each house, while preserving that option for future residents.

The characteristics of these shell-dwellings were: common width frontage, avoidance of internal load bearing walls, and judicious positioning of wet services. This allowed interiors to be organised in different ways. Individual preferences are evident in the variety of floor plans, many with different arrangements of storage space, often adding to the effective size of the living room, but always complying with the required Parker Morris Standards.

Staircase arrangements and utility room provision show marked individual differences, and kitchens have been personalised in arrangement and colour schemes. Stairs can be enclosed at any time and statutory access to the garden is provided by a path at the rear of each house.

The unusual 'thrust' porch, suggested by the architects and taken up by co-op members, removes the lobby from the living room, enlarging this space and allowing many more types of furniture arrangement.

Final verdicts

Insight into the final results can be gained from what members now have to say about the project and how it was carried out, as quoted in an article 'Members' views' in *Architects' Journal* (18 July 1984).

Alan Hoyle, first chairman of the co-op, felt the main value of the project was the 'power to the people bit'. In his view, the scheme demonstrated that if ordinary people were given the reins, they could produce 'a really excellent housing scheme'. The main obstacle was overcoming the unwillingness of people to make design decisions, after years of 'professional disabling'. Hoyle felt that the Parker Morris Standards constituted an obstacle to full participatory design, since they were made to protect standards which members would have protected themselves in more appropriate ways. He emphasised that a good, co-operative working relationship with the architectural team was necessary for a project like this to succeed.

Joan Fisher, secretary of the co-op, felt a very important achievement was to have avoided the 'Victorian working-class look', and that the project had achieved three-quarters of what members wanted from it.

Elaine Dutton, member of the design committee, was pleased with the colourfulness of the exteriors and the general design, although she pointed out that some future problems and potential dangers (especially to do with children playing on the court and grounds) had not been foreseen. However, because of the co-operative nature of the project, steps could be quickly taken to correct them.

Another member, Mary Waring, stressed the community spirit

that the scheme had inspired, and the positive experience that learning to shape their environment, and actually doing it, had been for all concerned: 'I'd go through the time and effort again. It was worth every minute.'

The Hesketh Street Housing Co-operative project has been praised by a number of prominent housing institutions and individuals. It received the Housing Centre Trust Jubilee Commendation of 1984, and the Town Planning Institute Commendation for 'Outstanding Achievement' in the same year. The project has also been visited and praised by the Prince of Wales, who has become a public defender of co-operative housing design and management, and by the Secretary of State for the Environment.

The history since

As the Hesketh Street Co-operative project was in progress, the shifting sands of Liverpool politics brought about some very important changes. In 1975, after many years of Labour hegemony, the Liberal Party was brought to power in the local elections. In spite of a waiting list of 12,000 families, the new council put a stop to all new building, and concentrated resources on the rehabilitation of the existing stock, much of it old tenement blocks. Some funding was also offered for the repair of sub-standard private housing in General Improvement Areas. Under this programme several housing co-ops were formed to rehabilitate older properties. By 1978, however, it was evident that rehabilitation was not enough, and some tenements and old terraces would have to come down and rehousing provided. Rather than build directly, the council encouraged the setting up of new-build housing co-ops, to rehouse families from clearance areas. The council agreed to fund six such groups, and a new era of 'enablement' (albeit with minimal funding) seemed to be beginning.

The 'co-op spring' was soon over. In 1983 Labour regained power, with a Bevanite programme of extending municipal services. The programme included the building of 3,600 houses, and the repair, improvement and conversion of a further 7,000 by 1988. The programme had a cost of £265 million, to be funded from rates and the DoE (a suggestion that the DoE strongly rejected). The building programme would be developed on traditional Garden City lines, although ready-built new housing would also be purchased. It would be managed by the council, and would employ private consultants and contractors as well as local authority development and management staff, creating an additional 1,000 jobs.

Participatory design and co-operative management found no place within this programme. Co-ops with council-funded projects under way were told they would be 'municipalised', the functions of allocation and management to be taken over by the council. New co-ops were told that no further funding would be available.

The local Labour Party's position on co-ops was particularly doctrinaire – they considered co-ops to be an attack on municipal housing, and a threat to its continued funding. They were adamant that only direct provision and management by the council would provide the quantity and quality of housing needed by the working-class. Co-ops were dismissed as peripheral, and 'middle-class'. They were said to 'house a category of tenant we would not give priority to' and anyway were 'a Tory/SDP plot to undermine council housing'.

In June 1983, the tenants of Liverpool's housing co-ops marched in protest at the council's policies. Individual members of co-ops joined local groups of the Labour party and argued the case for their organisations. But all this came too late, and was too sporadic. Most co-op members had little experience of political organisation, and little spare time. Some were worried about blacklisting by municipal authorities. People on the waiting list, who might have benefited from co-ops, had little opportunity to find out about them, and so had little alternative to the offical programme.

As background to this local confrontation was the major political battle between the council and the government. The council was charged with unauthorised spending of £177 million on its service programme (80 per cent of which was attributable to penalties for 'overspending'). Councillors were threatened with further surcharges, disqualification and even arrest. Housing co-ops provided yet another brick to throw at the 'Militant' council, and much enthusiasm for them was suddenly shown in quarters where it had never previously been evident.

The positive side of this was to encourage the government to put more Housing Corporation funds (at a time of cutbacks), into Liverpool co-ops. The negative side was to push co-ops, nominally at least, into the ranks of the opposition. They were lumped together with Conservative 'steps to private ownership' housing initiatives, and dubbed 'anti-council housing'. But co-operatives have traditional roots in the Labour movement, and were not prepared to be so easily disowned. In other cities, like Glasgow, Labour Councils had co-operated with co-operatives in the rehabilitation and management of council estates. The Labour Party nationally decided to get involved. Jeff Rooker MP, Labour Shadow Housing Minister, whilst introducing a new Labour housing policy document, stated:

> To refer to co-operators as elitist is an abuse of the language. When I spent a day a couple of months ago with half a dozen or so housing co-ops in Liverpool I did not meet one co-operator who was not authentic working class, and most were unemployed. It *is* elitist to think experts, officers, councillors and, yes, MPs, know best. It is the people who know best. Our task is to provide the resources, the legal framework, and above all the political will to upset the existing order so that people can decide.

These sentiments, and other suggestions put forward in the policy document, if implemented, would represent the beginning of a real shift in Britain's housing policies to public enablement, as a complement to provision.

Meanwhile, the Labour Group on Liverpool Council has been mostly disqualified from holding office for refusing to set a rate within government guidelines. Because of this, the Liberal group returned briefly to power, but by government, rather than popular decree. Recent local elections have given the Labour party control again. Co-ops continue to develop, but it is hard to see the rift between them and the Labour movement healing in the near future.

Summary

Hesketh Street Housing Co-operative is a good example of how a community can be organised, and 'enabled', to control the design, construction and subsequent management of its own housing. This project produced good quality dwellings, tailored to the needs and preferences of individual occupiers, while working with public funds, to similar cost limits and standards as conventional council housing.

Capital funding for the project came from central government (through the Housing Corporation's HAG arrangements), and additional funding for co-operative education was available from the same source. Revenue funding (for management and maintenance) came from individual rents paid by co-op members, fixed at Fair Rent levels.

Land was provided by the council (during a period of co-operation with housing association development). The plot used was ideally suited to the group and the project, although it was probably a coincidence that it was offered to CDS at that time.

Works on drains and roads within the project were contracted out by the co-op, under administrative and technical supervision of CDS and the architects. Some council intervention was required on drains, and this led to a degree of delay. The project was designed and built to Parker Morris Standards, and expenditure limited by the cost-yardstick. Because of these limitations a number of items had to be deleted from the final works schedule by the co-op. Works were delayed an extra 12 months due to Housing Corporation cutbacks, but the extra time was usefully employed in finalising design and in co-operative education.

The co-op itself was formed by the amalgamation (through CDS) of two separate groups, both of which approached CDS because of its proven track record and willingness to help co-operative initiatives. CDS performed the role of an effective development agent: after bringing the group together, it helped it obtain legal status, and followed this up with a comprehensive education programme. This programme included the information required to make financial, technical and management decisions. CDS also showed the co-op the range of architectural services available, and how it could ensure that architects worked to its requirements. It briefed architects to make sure they knew what the co-op expected of them.

The architects took over where CDS left off. They explained to the co-op the range of design and building options open to it (within current standards and cost-limits) and the different materials that could be used. They took participation beyond individual house design, to exterior design and landscaping. They helped the co-op select builders who could produce the desired effects.

Financial and legal procedures were dealt with by CDS, which kept the co-op informed on possible alternatives. Technical supervision was in the hands of the architects, who acted on the co-op's instructions.

The role of the various government bodies was limited to providing land, providing funding and monitoring its use, and providing the legal framework in which the project could develop, and the standards and cost-limits which applied. Although these were not always ideal, they were adequate, and the only major interference with the project's development was the government's erratic funding of the Housing Corporation.

In contrast to the other case histories, housing at Hesketh Street is collectively owned by the co-op. It cannot be sold to individual members, and they do not hold shares in individual properties. The co-op has been granted the entire capital funding for the project by the DoE through the Housing Corporation, needing only to raise a small 'residual mortgage' out of rent income. The rest of the rent income is available to the co-op to fulfil its 'landlord' role, managing and maintaining the properties. The co-op has chosen to contract out part of this responsibility to CDS (which has a professional management section), while keeping overall control. The co-op is also responsible for allocation and re-allocation of properties, although it gives the council nomination rights.

The fundamental difference between this and other housing models, is that a separate user-organisation has been directly financed from public funds, rather than money going to individual members or development bodies. Given control of capital and revenue finance, the user-group could therefore demand that architects and builders, and to a lesser degree development and management agents, work to its requirements.

Instrumental in this variation was the existence of an effective secondary agency. Without CDS (or an organisation like it) it is unlikely that the co-op could have formed, or have been funded. Secondary development agencies are therefore essential to the operation of this model, and will require extra funding (apart from income derived from development and management functions) to fulfil their functions effectively.

The 'inversion' of the usual model of housing provision puts the onus on development agents, architects and builders to work in a more open, participatory manner. This in turn stimulates the search for new methods of making this participation effective (often involving innovative techniques), which are valuable contributions

	Cost per m² £	Percent of total %
Preliminaries and insurances	7.67	3.77
Work below lowest floor finish	23.49	11.59
Structural elements		
Upper floors	8.64	4.25
Roof	19.99	9.86
Staircases	3.99	1.96
External walls	20.12	9.93
Windows and external doors	12.33	6.05
Internal walls	6.60	3.25
Partitions	6.16	3.03
Internal doors	6.66	3.28
Ironmongery	2.18	1.07
Total of structural elements	86.62	42.69
Finishes and fittings		
Wall finishes	9.05	4.45
Floor finishes	6.65	3.27
Ceiling finishes	3.40	1.67
Decoration	8.51	4.19
Fittings	4.85	2.38
Total of finishes and fittings	32.46	15.96
Services		
Sanitary appliances waste, soil and overflow pipes, cold and hot water services, heating, ventilation and gas services	27.57	13.60
Electrical services	5.71	2.81
Drainage	19.42	9.58
Total of services	52.70	25.99
Total	202.94	100.00

Building cost   £654,268
External works £170,668

1. Foundation costs were increased by the use of a concrete raft where previous foundations could not be excavated.
2. Roofs were insulated, but not cavity walls, and no double glazing was provided.
3. Services at 26 per cent of the cost, which is above average for this type of scheme, due to high drainage costs and the fact that services could not be totally centralised to allow variation in design. Houses are equipped with full central heating, prefabricated plumbing units, boilers and hot water units.
4. Overall building costs are £203 per square metre, which is reasonable for a city scheme containing 40 per cent flats. Building cost per bedspace is £5,592, or £7,050 including external works.
5. 26 per cent was allowed for external costs, showing the importance of exteriors and grounds.
6. These costs do not take into account the hidden cost to members, architects and CDS, in terms of evening meetings and extra paperwork, as a result of the participatory methods used.

Costs of Hesketh Street Housing Co-operative.

to housing practice.

This model has many advantages over conventional public provision. Although the apparatus of council housing is in theory democratic, it suffers from the shortcomings of any parliamentary system. Democracy is often limited to the election of councillors (on the basis of abstract policies and promises) and there is no effective way of determining individual needs or preferences of people using the services. Building decisions are therefore made on abstract ideological grounds (such as the ubiquitous Garden City), or on scientific or financial considerations. In practice, decisions are often left up to non-elected civil servants. Because they control funding, architects will design for them, and builders will come up with whatever construction systems they require at the time. These rarely coincide with real user needs and preferences.

A further disadvantage of exclusive direct management of public housing by councils is that the council housing apparatus periodically falls into the hands of political groups which, far from representing the tenants, are inimical to the principles of the provision. Public housing is thus run down, or sold off (or both) without occupiers being able to do much about it. This could have been avoided by establishing co-operative user-control of public housing from the start. This option has not been explored, partly because of the powerful interests in favour of more conventional forms of provision, partly because of the polarisation of housing alternatives into council housing *or* owner-occupation. There is reason to hope, however, that the policies of major parties are now changing to incorporate measures to facilitate public 'enablement' of community housing initiatives, and community control of public housing.

7 | A co-operative council in Glasgow

Scotland's entrenched feudalism did its best to discourage the growth of Glasgow – 16th century burgh boundaries limited its sprawl and 'feu duties' taxed would-be urban developers. But the town's favourable situation on the banks of the Clyde was too strong an attraction for merchants and industrial entrepreneurs. Waves of rural migrants from Central Scotland, Ireland, the Highlands and the Isles soon provided the human foundations for the building of engineering firms such as Beardmore's, Parkhead, Dixon's Blazes, Govanhill, Fairfields and Stephen's shipyards in Govan. The textile industry also blossomed.

With them came the characteristic Glasgow tenement. Needing to come up with a solution to the restrictions on land use and the land tax, would-be developers turned a cosmopolitan eye to Italy, Germany and Holland, where the tenement-style building was commonplace. Maximising both income and land use, the tenement also used sandstone, which was locally abundant. The first tenements were recorded as early as 1600. At the end of the 18th century, the first tenement estate was built for the weavers of New Lanark. Between 1861 and 1891 Glasgow's housing stock increased from 86,600 to 140,800 dwellings – mostly working-class housing of this sort.

The typical block was four storeys, with as many as 16 flats, only accessible through a central staircase. Facilities in the flats were minimal, with usually one or two rooms and no separate cooking facilities. The backyard provided a shared washroom and toilet, and some space for craft workshops. The tenement allowed a concentration of humanity which earned Glasgow the reputation for being 'the most crowded city in Western Europe'. The handful of landlords that owned most of the tenements found them ideally suited – the tenants were not as fortunate. Apart from overcrowding, they lacked light, fresh air and sanitary facilities.

In Thomson's Building in Orr Street, 54 families shared one outside toilet. With conditions like these, it is hardly surprising that the cholera epidemics of 1848 and 1853 claimed nearly 7,000 victims.

In 1857 and 1859, committees were established to look into public health in Glasgow. They concluded that only municipal intervention could enforce tolerable conditions. They recommended giving authorities powers to clear and demolish. They also suggested the setting up of a City Improvement Trust, to make land available for urban development while enforcing minimum housing standards. This Trust was also authorised to build. These recommendations were made law by the Glasgow Improvement Act of 1866. But by 1914 the weakness of these measures was evident – 16,000 dwellings had been demolished, but only 2,199 built by the Trust. Also, private developers using Trust land had largely disregarded the required 'minimum standards'.

Few initiatives from the voluntary sector are recorded during this time. The Glasgow Workingmen's Dwellings Company Ltd attempted to prove that housing development to acceptable standards was possible at current 'slum' rentals. They soon owned hundreds of houses, many of which they had built directly, but many of which, being old tenements, they had bought and renovated. But as *Miles Better, Miles to Go*, an account of Glasgow housing associations, describes, their allocation policies reveal a less admirable, but not unusual attitude:

> While retaining old tenants as far as possible, the directors have hitherto in their reconstructions preferred to overhaul and renovate the properties thoroughly at the start, allowing to return to their old homes only tenants who seem anxious to reform, and are likely to make good use of their opportunities.

Less information is available about early co-operative ventures in Glasgow, such as the Fairfields Co-op in Govan, built to house local shipyard workers. These no doubt faced the same financial limitations that affected their English counterparts. But on the whole it was the profit motive that produced them, and until the middle of this century they were the domain of the private landlord.

The saving grace of the tenements was that they allowed communities to form and survive. The people housed were often already linked by family, cultural and religious ties. They usually shared a common workplace. This process of natural allocation created tightly-knit neighbourhood communities which were often able to understand and fight for their common interests. The solidarity of these working-class communities helped shape the reputation of the 'Red Clyde'. Many years later Harry McShane, a union organiser, remembered:

> The South Side, Govan and Gorbals, was a very lively place for socialist propaganda. We sold literature, we held meetings, and, for a big event, we bill-posted everywhere. You couldn't walk through without seeing the pavement chalked with socialist slogans. (*No Mean Fighter*, Joan Smith)

The first decade of the 20th century brought the housing problem in Glasgow to a head. Rising building costs and increased municipal intervention since the 1866 Act had deterred further private building. At the same time, the growing drive to re-arm was multiplying work opportunities in shipbuilders and factories. Migrant workers swarmed to the city, pushing up rents and fostering further overcrowding. A Commission set up to look at industrial housing in Scotland had concluded:

> Private enterprise had failed to keep pace with demand, and . . . the State alone, operating through local authorities, was able to take up the responsibility.

By 1914 many Glaswegians had been called up to fight in the Great War, leaving wives and families in the tenements. These 'soldiers' wives' were hardly in a position to meet spiralling rent increases, so were in the front line for harassment and eviction by slum landlords. Outrage amongst tenement women at this practice led to the creation of the Glasgow Women's Housing Association in Govan. This organisation won the support of Glasgow tenants by a daring combination of direct action and political campaigning. They also gained the support of the shipyard workers and Glasgow Trades Council, and of the Scottish Independent Labour Party. But their most significant action was the Glasgow Rent Strike of 1915, when 25,000 tenants were persuaded to withhold rents until an official inquiry was agreed. The government in London rushed through the first Rent Restriction Act, stabilising rents at the 1914 level. As a result of this campaign, working-class housing in

Glasgow and Britain was never quite the same again.

In 1917 the Royal Commission on Housing in Scotland emphasised the continuing overcrowding in Glasgow with the following figures:

No. of occupants per room:	Glasgow	Average English city
More than 4	10.9%	0.8%
More than 3	27.9%	1.5%
More than 2	55.7%	9.4%

Glasgow's municipal housing

It was a Conservative administration in the city which pioneered municipal housing in Glasgow, in 1919. The first schemes, more predictably, were aimed at the better-off skilled and white collar workers. They were the peripheral garden suburbs, mainly cottages and terraces, with a thoughtful provision of open spaces and local amenities. Knightswood and Mosspark were examples of this.

Less attractive schemes with lower rentals, such as Blackhill in East Glasgow, were also built close to industrial centres. As with later developments, they were notably lacking in amenities. Regarding the principles that were thus established for Glasgow's municipal housing, Duncan Maclennan, Director of the Centre for Housing Research at Glasgow University, comments that:

> The development of public housing – with the implicit assumption that new peripheral public housing was always better for all individuals than core area public housing – has dominated housing in Scotland for more than 50 years.

In 1933 Labour took power in Glasgow, putting their weight behind municipal housing. With brief interludes they have held control to this day. In total, between the two wars, 54,289 houses were built using public funds, contrasted with only 9,106 built independently by private developers. Not surprisingly, by 1981, 64 per cent of housing in Glasgow was municipally owned.

After the Second World War the 'municipal blitz' hit the tenements. As the historian William Fergusson pointed out:

What Hitler so markedly failed to achieve in the 1940s, Glasgow Corporation cheerfully carried out in the following decades in the name of progress.

Ten per cent of the city's population was cleared from inner city areas and rehoused in new peripheral estates like Easterhouse, Castlemilk and Drumchapel. Being built for quantity and speed, these new estates were typically made up of five-storey blocks, and lacked essential amenities. Communities forged in the struggle in the tenements were dispersed, to make way for high-rise blocks, built to higher densities than had previously been allowed anywhere in Britain. With hindsight, even the tenement seemed preferable. Harry McShane commented that: 'In terms of social considerations and human happiness, the old tenement area offers a great deal more than the council estate.'

At the time, however, residents were glad to leave these stone warrens. Apart from overcrowding and lack of sanitary facilities, inner Glasgow at the time lived under a blanket of smog. The new estates offered internal toilets, large kitchens, and the possibility of 'clean air'. Their worrying isolation from social amenities and potential employment was countered with assurances of plentiful cheap transport. It took a few years before the message got through. By that time those with work were trying their best to move to more favourable locations, and those without work were rapidly losing hope. The council compounded the hopelesness by practically ignoring the tenants, not giving them any basis for organisation or participation in the running of the estate. The council was a faceless landlord who regularly collected the rent and occasionally carried out repairs.

In 1957, the blitz centred on the older areas of the city. Twenty-nine Comprehensive Development Areas (CDAs) were singled out for clearance, demolition and redevelopment. The problems that ensued were of a similarly massive scale.

The difficulties of co-ordinating such a programme, the complicated sequence of bureaucratic procedures, plan submissions, compulsory purchase orders, public inquiries and plan approvals, the lack of co-ordination between clearance and rehousing criteria, and between demolition and redevelopment, led to acres of vacant sites and blighted homes, and hundreds of tenants abandoned in half-empty, derelict tenements. On the other hand the refugees of the blitz were begining to discover the shortcomings of their new 'peripheral' environments.

Perhaps because of their traditional loyalty to Labour, or because they could not see the consequences of these housing policies, the communities of the Clyde did little to resist these moves. Only the scale of the clearance programme prevented further damage being done: by 1973, of 29 suggested CDAs only 9 had been cleared.

Community-based housing associations

The decision to change course came from the inside Glasgow. Demolition and high-rise redevelopment were becoming unpopular nationally, partly because of the rising cost of new building in relation to rehabilitation. Also, the government's decision to make additional funding available to housing associations working in inner city improvement helped. But there was another factor, as a Glasgow District Council official pointed out:

> Of much greater importance was a 'gut' feeling – experienced by many members as well as officers – that enough was enough as far as large-scale redevelopment was concerned.

Enlightened sentiments like these brought with them a new role for the voluntary sector. Since the Glasgow Workingmen's Dwelling Company, few housing associations had contributed to the city's low-income housing. The spark for change came from the work of final-year architectural students at Strathclyde University. In 1969 one, Raymond Young, carried out research work into the technical aspects of tenement improvement. Another, Jim Johnson, went to live in Govan, to see if such improvements could actually be implemented by a community. With the support of the Architecture Department of the university and the largely middle-class New Govan Society, they proposed a Tenement Improvement Programme (TIP) for the area. Their proposal was that the council should support owner-occupiers in the area in rehabilitating their properties rather than having them demolished. In 1971, they gained municipal support for this proposal.

TIP's objective was not primarily to introduce housing associations into Govan. According to one of its members:

> Our main concern was to influence the local authority to operate differently – by taking account of the interests of local residents, by establishing a more participatory approach and by accepting the feasibility of a more sensitive approach to rehabilitation.

However, housing associations were seen as the most appropriate vehicle for achieving this aim. In 1971, on the advice of TIP, representatives of various Govan community groups registered the Central Govan Housing Association (CGHA), with the aim of purchasing property from private owners who did not wish to carry out improvements themselves. But CGHA's first scheme was in fact the short-life repair of a block of dwellings in Taransay Street, which had been bought by the council for a proposed motorway. TIP acted as development agent and architect to the scheme, and CGHA took the properties under management. It was quite an undertaking. One of CGHA's committee members commented:

> At the beginning, we were told 'It's your association' and 'You are in control'. No-one told us we would be responsible for the equivalent of a business spending millions of pounds a year; that we would be monitored closely by local people and by government bodies; that we would employ more than ten professional staff working in three departments and depend on the work of contractors and consultants.

In 1972, TIP received further backing from the Scottish Development Department (SDD) at the Scottish Office and a charitable trust, and became ASSIST, a city-wide professional services agency, promoting the community-based renovation of tenements throughout Glasgow. A second community-based housing association (CBHA) was set up in Govanhill in 1973. Others were to follow. But the real boost to CBHAs came in 1974, with new legislation that channelled substantial funding to housing associations, under the auspices of the Housing Corporation. Glasgow council welcomed this development, and began attempting to co-ordinate its urban renewal programme with the local office of the Housing Corporation.

From 1974 to 1980, 21 CBHAs were registered in Glasgow. There was a honeymoon period, when the council and the Housing Corporation worked hand-in-glove on tenement rehabilitation. The local authority undertook to survey properties where rehabilitation was proposed, so that associations could gauge the scale of the repair required. Houses were purchased by the council and held until a housing association was available to buy them. The Housing Corporation set up a legal service to help associations in the intricacies of purchasing properties.

But this relationship was soon soured by clashes over the cost-limits set by the Scottish Development Department and enforced by the Housing Corporation. CBHAs found these limits unrealistic, and felt they disregarded the particular difficulties of tenement rehabilitation, and that they could not be implemented without creating unacceptably low standards. CBHAs therefore felt obliged to submit schemes which were over cost limits, which the Housing Corporation then had to pass on to the SDD for approval. This was called 'double scrutiny', and resulted in long delays in approval that frustrated tenants and staff, as one member explained:.

> By the time we were off and running with our first scheme finished and a good programme in the pipeline, we hit problems with cost limits, and then delays when every scheme had to get approval from Edinburgh.

Due to such clashes, the Housing Corporation came to be viewed less as a supportive partner in urban redevelopment and a nurturing body for the CBHAs, and more as an instrument of central government control of housing policy. In 1978 the CBHAs formed a regional federation called the Glasgow Forum of Housing Associations, and organised a lobby of Parliament. This body has been active in campaigning for a better deal for Glasgow associations to this day.

John Patterson, vice-chairman of Govanhill Housing Association, gives this view of the struggle. (It can be sung to the tune of *These Are My Mountains*):

> Community housing is something worthwhile
> The tenement buildings now have plenty o' style
> We're no really braggin', it's there to be seen
> The auld 'But and Ben' type is now just a dream

We've noo modernised them and made them sae braw
Although I must tell you, some are a bit sma'
But I don't think it matters, the folk like them fine
So please Mr Younger just give us more time

So come a' ye members, committees an' a'
That bide here in Glasgow the Toon we've made braw
Mair money is needed tae rehab the trash
So please Mr Hastie just give us the cash

Of course there's the Forum, who show us the light
An the Toon's Federation keep the legal side right
Our members keep trying yet sometimes we're sad
But we're never doonhearted, an our records no' bad.

(Sir George Younger was Secretary of State for Scotland at the time, and James Hastie was Director of the Housing Corporation in Scotland.)

Tenant management co-ops

As a result of the recommendations of the Campbell Working Party into co-operative housing, an amendment was included in the 1975 Housing Rent and Subsidies Act, which made the setting up of tenant management co-operatives in council estates possible. In Harold Campbell's own words:

> It gave powers to a local authority to enter into an agreement with any group of its tenants who chose to form themselves into a registered co-operative association to act under paid contract as managing agents for the estate in which they live.

Glasgow District Council was already pursuing a pragmatic investigation into the advantages of participation. So it required no major change in policy to set up the city's first tenant management co-op in the new Summerstown estate in 1976. New tenants from clearance areas were given a choice of going into council-managed housing, or opting for one of the co-op's 247 dwellings.

In Summerstown, the council developed their own particular

model for a tenant management co-op. Rents (which were higher than council rents) were collected by the local authority, and although the co-op chose its own maintenance contractors, the council made the payments. If the co-op spent less than the yearly allowances allocated to it for management and maintenance of the dwellings, they were free to use the surplus to carry out additional improvements to the estate. The co-op could also use management allowances to employ an administrative worker through the council. Since the co-op had no independent financial existence, it did not need to register as a Friendly Society nor with the Housing Corporation.

A survey by the SDD of the residents of Summerstown co-op showed they were mainly young skilled workers with families. On the whole they were satisfied with the estate, particularly with those aspects of management that were under their direct control (such as refuse collection). Through their efforts they had accumulated a surplus in the management and maintenance account, which they were intending to use for improvements. The report stated:

> The co-operative has proved very effective at management of day-to-day issues in a sensitive and practical way. The management of repairs is one of the best examples.

On the other hand, the survey revealed that participation was low. Although a strong sense of community had evolved, a year and a half after formation most tenants were still unclear as to how the co-operative operated. Instead, they relied on a small, dedicated management committee. This worried the professionals, but not the members:

> It has become apparent every time from Summerstown and the other co-operatives elsewhere that achievements which may satisfy members may be different from professional concepts of success.

In 1980, the council took participation a step further by setting up a co-op in an already-tenanted estate. This was the Spiers Management Co-op in Yoker. In Spiers the tenants themselves supervised the rehabilitation of their run-down and hard-to-let

estate, using similar methods to those developed by the CBHAs.
Together with their architects, they took decisions on internal
arrangements of flats, kitchen layouts and heating arrangements.
By 1983 Glasgow boasted five more tenant management co-
operatives: Caldercuilt, Invershiel and Whiterose managing council-
owned stock; Fairbridge and Claythorne managing properties
owned by the Scottish Special Housing Association.

The community ownership programme

It is possible that Glasgow would have stopped short of actually
handing over ownership of council housing to co-operatives, had
it not been for overriding financial factors. As early as 1979, in
a report entitled *Alternative Housing Strategy*, the council had
drawn attention to the state of disrepair of its housing stock. It
warned of the impossibility of adequately repairing or upgrading
its 180,000 dwellings, due to a continuing reduction in the Housing
Support Grant provided by central government. It recommended
urgent measures to involve tenants in determining what the few
resources available should be used for, and in harnessing private
funds, and funds intended for the private sector, in the repair of
this stock.

Typical conditions in the estates were described in a report by
Jean Stead for *The Guardian*:

> Tenants cannot heat their homes because architects installed
> expensive underfloor electric heating systems. Now the council
> cannot afford to carry out repairs. Leaking roofs compound the
> disaster. On estates where half the tenants are out of work, they
> heat one room for a few hours at a time with a one-bar electric
> fire.

The crunch came towards the end of 1983. The SDD announced
that it was cutting Glasgow's Housing Support Grant to half its
1981 level. The council estimated it needed £86 million just to keep
its housing windproof and watertight. The government was only
prepared to allow it £56 million. To make up the shortfall, the
government recommended that Glasgow put its council rents up
by 23 per cent. Paul Mugnaioni, Glasgow's Housing Director

commented:

> It shows a ludicrous lack of policy. No self-respecting business person would ever consider this approach to a product, putting up the price while they let it run down in quality.

Around this time the council apparently approached the Housing Corporation to see if their funds could be used to remedy the situation. But a lifeline was not forthcoming at this point. The council therefore proposed a desperate alternative: that of 'privatising' some of the worst-hit estates under 'community ownership'. Thus funds intended for the private sector could be used to carry out much-needed repairs and improvements.

For an instrument to make this possible the council again turned to the voluntary sector. Tenants in the worst-hit estates could form 'par value co-operatives', and these co-operatives could be sold the estates at reduced rates, securing private mortgages for this purpose. The council would then provide a variety of grants to allow rehabilitation both of the housing and of the area. The mortgages would be subsidised by tax relief, and tenants would be eligible for housing benefit on rents paid to the co-op after rehabilitation.

The model of the par value co-op (meaning simply a co-operative where every member holds an equal stake), was chosen for a number of reasons: every member's share was limited to £1, ensuring democratic control; if the co-operatives became 'fully mutual' (where every member was a tenant or a prospective tenant), community control of the housing would be assured: and if such a co-op became registered with the Housing Corporation then tenants would lose the Right to Buy, guaranteeing that the houses remained in the public sector.

An initial sounding-out of demand for the programme brought an overwhelming response. Fourteen tenant organisations from all over Glasgow indicated their interest in being involved. Some had already gone some way towards forming tenant management co-operatives, but had seen planned improvements aborted by expenditure cuts.

After a preliminary study of those interested, the council gave the go-ahead for four detailed feasibility studies: Calvay Crescent in Barlanark, Ballanatay in Castlemilk, Broomhouse in Baillieston and Wellshot in Cambuslang. Later, under pressure, it approved three more, to be known as the 'second-stage' co-ops: Priesthill, Southdene in Drumchapel and Possil. The council agreed to underwrite the cost of these feasibility studies.

Each of the seven schemes was asked to appoint a steering committee to develop its project, liaising with consultants – selected by each steering committee – and the council through a council-appointed liaison officer.

Calvay Housing Co-operative

To the east of Glasgow, just outside Easterhouse, lies the sprawling post-war estate of Barlanark. The estate was built at the time of Glasgow's tenement clearances, when emphasis was on the rapid provision of large quantities of housing, built to high space standards (in terms of square footage), but with few complementary amenities. There are a total of 8,000 flats in the estate.

The area proposed for the co-op was situated between Barlanark Road and Calvay Road, including Calvay Crescent, an area comprising 366 flats and six shop units. A vacant two-storey house was also situated within the area, with a sector of open land between the two roads. A survey of the area at the time indicated that 75 per cent of all breadwinners were unemployed, and there were few local employment opportunities, due to the absence of amenities such as pubs, libraries and shops.

About this time, Greenwich Council in London organised a tenants' study tour of Glasgow co-ops, and the resulting report commented on this estate:

> Situated miles away from any major centre, with neither pub, community facilities, doctor, public transport nor hardly any shops, the estate is also in a very exposed location (it was cold and wet and windy enough for us, and this was May). Faulty design is evident everywhere – flats are crowded closely together, yet there are large overgrown courts between the blocks; there is no proper rubbish facility, and no caretaking, so rubbish is strewn everywhere; most flats have problems with damp and condensation; noise insulation between the flats is poor, and only one room has any heating provided.

Because of all these factors, the estate was generally considered a 'dumping ground'. There were many applications for transfers, and few new tenants were willing to move into the estate. Few housing points were required for tenancies to be allocated there.

Formation

The first step towards the creation of a co-op was taken in January 1984. Barlanark tenants' committee, which was already respected as a result of various community campaigns, met with the local council member, a housing officer, and architectural consultants McGurn Logan Duncan and Opfer. This firm had recently carried out a successful tenement rehabilitation for the council. The tenants' committee agreed to investigate further the possibility of rehabilitating an area of Barlanark, on the basis of a local co-operative.

A week later, the proposal was discussed with some of the residents in Calvay Road. The council explained the possibilities of grant-funding a par value co-operative in order that the required improvements might be carried out. Finally a mass meeting was convened at Barlanark Hall, where the organisational and technical proposals were explained to 270 residents. How clear the proposal was at this stage is uncertain – apparently many were left with the impression they could buy their homes for £1. Towards the end of the meeting a show of hands was taken, and a mandate given for a steering committee elected from the floor to look into the viability of setting up a co-op.

In February, the steering committee of Calvay Co-op met. They elected a chairman and secretary, appointed consultants, and began working with them on the feasibility study, as had been approved by the council. Their brief was the formation of a par value co-operative, to take over full management and maintenance of the 366 flats and the surrounding areas. These would be repaired and improved on the basis of specifications agreed between the the architects and the co-op. These improvements would be managed by the co-op through the architects, and where works were completed would revert to the co-op's permanent management and maintenance.

Since this process required extensive consultation, the steering committee began setting up a network of representatives covering every close in the estate. Towards the end of the month, close representatives met and discussed the details of the proposed improvements. The committee also visited local CBHAs to learn from their methods and experiences. The dynamic approach of Yoker Housing Association in particular seems to have impressed the Calvay group.

Recommendations of the feasibility study

The feasibility study was presented to the council in December 1984, making the following comments and recommendations:

Community development. The consultants noted that the physical improvement of the estate would not in itself guarantee a permanent improvement of the area. They recommended a policy of 'integrated community development', where local services and enterprises would be promoted, generating investment and employment. This would need a lifting of current planning restrictions for the area.

The proposed repair programme would in itself begin this process, and possibly continue it on the basis of the co-op's need to provide ongoing maintenance of properties and gardens, but thought would have to be given to supporting further appropriate enterprises and services in the area.

Purchase. The District Valuer had initially proposed a selling price of £1,480 per dwelling. The architects had estimated a value of £500 each. A compromise was reached at £956 per dwelling, to be met entirely from a building society mortgage.

An indication of the enthusiasm of the committee at this point was that they hoped the flats would be purchased by January 1985. Nearly three years later that purchase had not been completed.

Environmental improvement. The consultants proposed relying on their earlier experience in Easterhouse for dealing with this aspect. Mainly, they would aim at making spaces 'manageable and defensible' by apportioning gardens, either to specific tenants or specific closes. Only areas which were of communal use would be managed by the entire co-op.

This was achieved firstly by giving use of the front and back gardens immediately surrounding each close to the corresponding ground floor flats. If the flats did not have front and rear garden access, it would be provided. Twenty five per cent of the dwellings would thus become garden flats, and they could be re-allocated (if necessary) to those most needing them and most able to cope with them.

Every close would also have a fenced garden area, which would be shared by the upper flats. Each garden would have clothes drying and refuse disposal facilities, and a mixture of hard and soft landscaping. The front gardens would also be tree-lined, and landscaping would create a 'robust but manageable environment' to discourage vandalism.

Pedestrian walk-ways would be re-routed, taking into account new territorial arrangements and facilities like bus-routes, and external lighting would be improved.

The funding for these works would come from 100 per cent council grants, to a maximum of £1,000 per dwelling. It was hoped these environmental improvements could begin in January 1985 and be completed by 1987.

Common repairs to buildings. To improve the external appearance of the buildings, a 'facelift', involving stone-cleaning, rendering and pointing would be carried out. Roofs, gutters and downpipes would be renewed, and chimneys replaced where required. Roof cavities would be insulated. Common balconies would be sub-divided, and in some cases enclosed to provide more habitable space.

A comprehensive 'kit of parts' would be selected to improve the exterior of the buildings. This would include doors and window frames, and allow for personal touches like window boxes. Ground-floor flats would be provided with decorative window louvres, which would also act as security screens. Stairs and entrances would be repaired and redecorated.

The funding for these works would come from 90 per cent council grants, to a maximum of £4,320 per dwelling. The rest would be funded from a building society loan. It was hoped that these repairs could begin in July 1985, and be finished by 1987.

Improvements to dwellings. Internal repairs were not prioritised by the first feasibility study. This seems surprising but is less so on investigation. The flats themselves had acceptable structural and space characteristics. They were solid and large, and roofs, on the whole, were not too bad. The main priority was obviously the neglected appearance and inappropriate design of the exteriors and common spaces. Also, since the extent of improvements to individual dwellings depended on the level of grant the council could provide, a matter not yet clarified, the architects saw no point in going into much detail.

As far as the residents were concerned, sound and thermal insulation were the most important areas to improve internally,

followed by extra heating and ventilation, the renewal of electric
and plumbing installations and new bathrooms and kitchens. The
blocks also contained many flats that had too many bedrooms, and
others that had too few, so a certain amount of reorganisation of
internal spaces was required.

If the council were successful in having the area declared a
Housing Action Area, improvement grants of up to 90 per cent
of the cost of works could be provided, to a maximum of £11,700
per dwelling. Should the Scottish Development Department refuse
approval for this, it would only be able to grant 50 per cent of the
cost of works, to a maximum of about £6,500 per dwelling. The
balance in both cases would have to be provided by mortgage
funding.

Residents were afraid that, should the higher level of grant not
be available, then the first casualty would be improved sound and
thermal insulation.

Because of the uncertainty of the funding arrangements, the
consultants were unable to estimate a start or finishing date for
these works.

Complementary works. The consultants noted the importance of
developing the play areas according to the real needs of the area.
The steering committee was asked to survey the different age
groups, and incorporate their requirements into the design of these
facilities. Funding would be sought from Urban Aid and possibly
the new Minister for Sport. Local voluntary labour might also be
available to build them.

The consultants also proposed the repair of the derelict two-
storey building in the area, known as The Minister's House, as
an administrative centre for the co-op. Funding for this might be
available from the council, Urban Aid, or the Manpower Services
Commission.

It was further suggested that the co-op take over six commercial
premises in the block, and refurbish them with a view to negotiating
new leases. This would ensure a more balanced variety of
businesses, perhaps including a pharmacy and a general store.

Scheduling of works. At the time of the feasibility study, only 27
out of 45 closes were fully behind the proposed improvements, with
the rest being indifferent and one or two residents opposing them.
Because of this it was considered necessary to carry out works on
a close-by-close basis, while at the same time trying to obtain full

support from those remaining.

Organisation. The consultants recommended that the co-op register with the Registrar of Friendly Societies as a non-mutual housing co-operative, and apply for registration with the Housing Corporation. Presumably fully mutual status would only be possible when all residents agreed to form part of the co-op. Although this registration would bring it under Corporation supervision, it would also give additional security to building societies providing mortgage funding to the co-op, and allow it to claim a grant for Corporation Tax under Section 93 of the Finance Act of 1965.

Although actual repair and improvement works would be managed by the architects, they recommended that the council should second a development officer to the co-op, to allow the council to participate more actively in the process. As works reached their conclusion, further staff should be appointed to deal with management and maintenance. It was also recommended that the Housing Department continue to advise the staff and committee of the co-op on management matters after handover.

The consultants proposed that the steering committee should discuss the project with the local statutory and voluntary bodies (such as the police and local community organisations), and incorporate their suggestions on the different aspects of the scheme.

Management and maintenance. All environmental and building repairs and improvements would be carried out with due regard to future management and maintenance, attempting to reduce it to a minimum, and removing any features that were known to cause maintenance problems. For this purpose, the maintenance records of the buildings would be carefully studied.

As a way of easing the burden of management, the council had agreed to continue collecting rents. It would charge 5 per cent of the rents collected for providing this service.

Statutory rights of members. Members of the co-op would lose the Right to Buy, which was not seen as a problem since it seemed very unlikely that any of them would want to exercise it. It was agreed that tenants' relatives would have rights of succession to the accommodation. It was also suggested that co-op members could remain on the council's waiting list for two years without losing points, in case they decided to leave the co-op during this time.

Financial summary

In order to get an idea of the financial transactions involved, it is useful to look at a simplified version of the costings (at January 1985):

Capital expenditure (main project only):	£
Purchase of properties (366 dwellings at £956 each):	350,000
Environmental improvements (366 at £1,000):	366,000
Fabric repairs (366 at £4,800):	1,756,800
House improvements (366 at £13,000):	4,758,000
Total:	7,230,800

Capital income:	£
Environmental grant (366 at £1,000):	366,000
Fabric repair grant (90% – 366 at £4,320)	1,581,120
House improvement grant (90% – 366 at £11,700)	4,282,200
Mortgage funding	1,001,480
Total:	7,230,800

It is apparent that the co-operative would have to secure a loan of just over one million pounds to carry out the project. However, if improvement grants could only be provided at the 50 per cent level, the loan would have to be £2,904,680.

In the feasibility study, two financial cash flows were presented: one where rents rose by 10 per cent on the 1st April 1985, and 10 per cent every year thereafter, and another where rents rose by 25 per cent to begin with, and 10 per cent per annum thereafter. In order to sustain the higher level of mortgage the co-op would have had to raise rents above the desired levels, or reduce the level of internal repairs.

Revenue for the first year would be as follows (figures rounded to nearest £):

			£
8 x 1 room flats at	£282 p.a. =		2,254
140 x 3	"	425 p.a. =	59,472
208 x 4	"	523 p.a. =	108,830
2 x 7	"	690 p.a. =	1,380
8 x 3	"	477 p.a. =	3,813

	£
	175,749
Less: 32 voids at £425 p.a.	13,594
	162,155
Less: 10% Provision	16,215
Total:	£145,940

Expenditure depended very much on the terms negotiated for the mortgage. At the time of the study it seemed likely that the co-op would secure finance at one per cent above base rates with a four-year interest-only period – with some deferral of the interest payments – and then 25 yearly repayments. On this basis it was likely to break even after the first year.

	£
Estimated management expenditure (£2,500 monthly – about £90 per dwelling per year)	30,000
Estimated maintenance and insurance expenditure (£4,000 monthly – about £144 per dwelling per year)	48,000
Rent collection fee (5% of £145,940)	7,297
Available for interest repayments	60,643
Total:	£145,940

By the time payments on capital would be required, income would have been uplifted by yearly increments. The funding was therefore roughly 'index-linked'. It is also worth noting that the management and maintenance levels projected are considerably lower than those used by HAG-funded co-operatives.

On the above basis the proposal was considered financially viable, as long as the required level of house improvement grant funding could be secured.

An official spanner in the works

There is no doubt that the tenants were enthusiastic about the proposals. It seemed an opportunity to turn a daily nightmare into a dream come true. The report of the Greenwich study tour described their attitude towards the proposed improvements:

> They showed us not what there is now, but what *will be*, as tenants have worked with a community architect for 18 months to draw up plans for a major refurbishment of the estate.

In May 1985 the council published an official endorsement of three of the four feasibility schemes originally commissioned. Only one, Wellshot, had been dropped after a meeting of residents voted against the proposals.

Not only did the council accept most of the requirements of the feasibility studies, but it actually improved on them in various ways. Among other things it agreed to try to secure grants at an even higher level than had been envisaged in the studies, in order to ensure that all essential repairs and improvements were carried out. It also agreed to give the co-op a promotional grant of £7,000, and to second development staff to the projects as soon as possible. On commencement of works, it agreed to act as development agents for the co-op, thereby saving the cost of VAT. It further agreed to underwrite all consultants' fees to progress each feasibility study to tender stage.

But there was one looming problem: the consent of the Scottish Office was required for the following transactions:
1. Selling the properties to the co-ops at below market prices.
2. Designating the areas as Housing Action Areas, in order be able to give improvement grants at the higher level.
3. Allowing the co-op tax relief under the MIRAS (Mortgage

Interest Relief At Source) scheme, under which the mortgage interest would be paid out net of income tax. For this, Inland Revenue consent would also be required.

4. Guaranteeing loans or mortgages undertaken by the co-ops.

5. Acting as development managers for the co-ops.

The proposals were therefore duly sent off to the SDD at the Scottish Office and the Inland Revenue for approval. Some time later, the feasibility studies of the second stage co-ops were presented to the council and similarly endorsed. Their details were also sent on to the SDD for consideration.

Finally, on 22nd October 1985, nine months after the proposed starting date for the first projects, the Scottish Office convened a meeting which included representatives from Glasgow District Council, the Housing Corporation, and Calvay, Broomhouse and Castlemilk East co-operatives. Members of Southdene, Priesthill and Possil were not invited, although appear to have attended unofficially. The main purpose of the meeting appears to have been to reject the proposals made by the council regarding its proposed community ownership initiative. The reasons for this rejection were given as follows:

a. *The transfer of property at less than market rates was not authorised.* Although discounts of up to 50 per cent were available for individual tenants, they were not considered applicable in these circumstances.

b. *Glasgow District Council had no powers to guarantee loans from a bank.* The Scottish Office was clearly disregarding the precedent of overdraft guarantees granted by innumerable local authorities all over Britain.

c. *The Scottish Office was unwilling to allow Housing Action Areas for improvement to be declared.* It was considered that there were 'insufficient grounds' to authorise this designation, since none lacked 'standard amenities' and most did not fall below the 'tolerable standard definition' in the 1974 Housing Act.

d. *The Scottish Office was not prepared to allow members of the co-operative to receive the double benefit of housing benefit and mortgage tax relief.* This again ignored the precedent of countless privately-financed co-ops in England.

Permission for the council to act as development agent for the co-ops was also refused.

There seemed little doubt that the DoE and the Scottish Office were not willing to let the proposals go ahead. Why? A variety of reasons have been suggested. The most likely one is that they saw the proposal as a way of getting round the restrictions placed on local authority spending, and potentially as a way of frustrating the government's drive to force the sale of council estates. In particular, a clause in the conditions of transfer required the properties to be sold back to the council should the co-op collapse. A suspicious mind could interpret this as a ploy to use private sector funding (mortgage and improvement grants) to repair housing stock that would eventually revert to the local authority.

Another consideration could have been the fact the co-ops were closely linked to a local authority, and a Labour one at that. A successful community ownership programme in Glasgow might help destroy the image of co-ops being 'popular flagships' against centralised 'tyrannical' local authorities, and could have shown how they could be useful complements for improving conditions.

But after the stick came the carrot

The Scottish Office was, however, willing to offer the three co-operatives that had been invited to the meeting the possibility of re-presenting their projects for normal HAG funding under the auspices of the Housing Corporation. With this aim, the Minister of State for Local Government and Environmental Services agreed to release an additional £9 million to the Corporation's regional budget.

Glasgow council, and the unofficial guests from the second stage co-ops, were obviously dismayed at the response. Although the three 'chosen' co-ops could probably now go ahead, the community ownership programme as such had been torpedoed, and Glasgow was left with the bill for months of abortive feasibility studies and three groups of very disappointed tenants.

To the council's credit they did not attempt to sway the chosen co-ops one way or another, realising that this might be the only chance that tenants would have to improve their lot. Glasgow council also pledged unconditional support for the remaining three co-ops, and set about devising an alternative funding package, but one that would not need Scottish Office consent. Instead of declaring the areas Housing Action Areas, the council would now declare Improvement Orders, under the Housing (Scotland) Act 1974, which would enable 90 per cent of £10,200 to be paid per flat. These payments would not require SDD approval under the

1980 Tenants' Rights (Scotland) Act. If banks or building societies were unable to fund acquisition (lacking council guarantees) the council would provide annuity arrangements which would cover acquisition costs, plus an additional 10 per cent top-up to take grants levels to 100 per cent. A considerable amount of subsidy could also be provided by the provision of free services: rent and rates collection, the secondment of development staff for a two-year period and free technical advice. Though these services would be free to the second stage co-ops, the first stage co-ops would have to pay a fee of about 5 per cent of rental income for the services provided.

The second stage co-ops, with full council support, set to work on a new package. It was another 18 months before they were successful. In May 1987 Michael Ancram, then Minister of Housing for Scotland, announced that the go-ahead had been given for work, involving the transfer of 1,100 homes, to begin. It was three years after the idea had first been put forward – and just a month before the General Election . . .

In the meantime, Calvay and the other first stage co-ops, with characteristic pragmatism, had decided to pursue their schemes through the Housing Corporation, though they were far from happy with the situation. They had a number of qualms:

– The increased control that the Housing Corporation would gain of the scheme and the co-op by virtue of its HAG funding. The Corporation would have powers to place Corporation officials on the committee, to dismiss individual committee members or whole committee, to wind up the co-op and transfer its assets to another housing association, if it was judged 'inadequate'.

– The questions raised earlier by the community-based housing associations that HAG cost-limits were insufficient to provide a thorough level of repair, and that attempting to work over cost-limits would lead to lengthy delays and friction with the Corporation.

– The fact that HAG required rents to be pegged at Fair Rent levels, which represented a percentage rise of 40 per cent, with higher yearly uplifts than had been envisaged in the council's proposals. For existing tenants these increases would be phased over three years, but for new tenants they would take effect immediately. Calavy co-op members felt that this would restrict access to the co-op to people who were in receipt of housing benefit, since anyone else would either be unable to meet the higher rent levels or, if they did have the income, they would probably attempt to secure better accommodation for the same rent. They felt this measure would make it impossible for them to create a fair social mix in the co-operative.

Having accepted the HAG option, the members of Calvay are seeing the positive aspects of it. Increased cost limits under HAG have allowed a higher level of internal repair than had been contemplated in the original proposals. Repairs now include full sound and thermal insulation, extra heating, new kitchens and bathrooms and even an entryphone system and television points in every flat. Also, the higher management and maintenance provision allowed by the HAG system will mean that an extra £100 per year will be available for the management and maintenance of each flat.

On 12th December 1986 Calvay Housing Co-op inaugurated the first converted close of eight flats. The ceremony was attended by the Minister for Local Government and Environmental Services. This is a part of the first phase of the rehabilitation programme which will encompass the 87 blocks that the co-operative now owns. The rest will be purchased during four subsequent phases. About 200 residents are now members, with less than 50 as yet unwilling to join (there are 120 voids – vacant dwellings). This means that the mutuality question has not been resolved, and the co-op is functioning as a non-mutual co-op with a number of resulting complications.

Apart from this, the HAG option has allowed the co-op to advance and develop. The Calvay committee has four sub-committees which are actively developing the various aspects of the project. One in particular, on community initiatives, has been looking into ways of generating employment, providing recreational activities, creating alternative facilities and generally improving the environment. Alternative sources of funding, such as the Manpower Services Commission and Urban Aid funding, have been tapped to this aim.

With success has come an element of fame in housing circles, and members of Calvay are now invited to speak at all kinds of conferences, as well as receiving visitors from all over the world. They are particularly proud of an RIBA award, presented by the Prince of Wales.

It is a fitting result. The report of the Greenwich study tour had commented:

The strongest impression we took away from Calvay was the pride, enthusiasm and self-respect of the people there. In spite of the immense effort still required, they were inspired and motivated by their vision of the future for the estate.

In Calvay the strength of that vision seems to have triumphed.

Summary

This case history shows how community-based housing organisations can become effective tools in the pursuit of the interests of working class communities, and work hand-in-hand with Labour local authorities in the pursuit of these interests. It also shows how central government support for these organisations can quickly become obstruction if such a harmony is achieved.

Glasgow has an unusual history of popular struggle and solidarity. The scores of rural immigrants who found shelter in its overcrowded tenements were often bonded by blood, religion and culture, as well as by their common economic dependency on the nascent industries. It is not surprising therefore that Glasgow should host perhaps the most successful urban social movement in modern Europe, whose decisive action was the Glasgow Rent Strike of 1915, recognised as one of the main incentives to the introduction of rent controls and municipal housing.

From that time on, the commitment of Glasgow's local authority to the direct provision of housing has been second to none. Beginning with the 'municipalist' Conservatives of 1919, through the first Labour council of 1933, Glasgow pursued and developed its characteristic style for public housing, mainly building 'peripheral estates', initially well laid out and self-contained on Garden City principles, but gradually becoming denser and less desirable as subsidies were reduced.

After the Second World War and Bevan's housing programme, it looked as if Ebenezer Howard's visions were at last to become the norm, through exacting building standards and generous subsidies of that time. But the Garden City, with its Georgian houses with gardens, crumbled before the financial stringencies of the 1950s, giving way to the apparently more cost-effective, high-rise Radiant City visualised by Le Corbusier.

In 1956 the Conservative government of the day limited subsidies for new building to the provision of rehousing for slum clearance. At the same time, other subsidies and relaxed building regulations encouraged higher densities. In Glasgow the council embraced clearance without hesitation, uprooting communities and destroying hundreds of old tenements on the older parts of the city. The victims of this blitz were rehoused in rapidly multiplying blocks of flats on the peripheral estates, or in the dizzy heights of inner-city tower blocks. Non-priority residents, usually older people with grown-up children, were left waiting in the ruins of semi-abandoned tenements until the red tape eventually unravelled to reveal their destination . . .

Professor Alice Coleman, author of *Utopia on Trial: Vision and Reality in Planned Housing*, says of this 'utopia':

> It was conceived in compassion but has been born and bred in authoritarianism, profligacy and frustration. It aimed to liberate people from the slums but has come to represent an even worse form of bondage. It aspired to beautify the urban environment, but has been transmogrified into the epitome of ugliness.

It must be said in defence of the Glasgow Labour Party that it did not take it long to realise that the dream had become a nightmare. By 1970, both for financial and political reasons, Glasgow abandoned its clearance policies. At this point it first saw the potential of housing associations as partners in urban renewal. Rather than oppose and obstruct them, as other Labour authorities had done, Glasgow saw, correctly, that there was more mileage in promoting them, and using the funding now available to the voluntary sector in pursuit of its overall policies.

With this in mind, the council availed itself of local community architects, and set about to create the housing association movement in the city. Tangible evidence of the wisdom of this move are today's community-based housing associations, which have renovated and preserved many of Glasgow's traditional tenements, and been relentless in their pursuit of central government funding for the renewal or rehabilitation of housing stress areas.

Within this new spirit of pragmatism, Glasgow council later formed tenant management co-ops on some of the estates, allowing residents themselves to decide how public resources should be used. But initiatives like this were soon curtailed by continuing cuts to its Revenue Support Grant, until the council was obliged to propose not only handing management of the estates over to the tenants, but ownership as well.

Calvay Housing Co-op was not initiated by the tenants. It was promoted by the council, who persuaded them that this was the best way to secure the upgrading of their estate. Consultants employed by the council guided the residents in organising themselves, determined financial feasibilities and consulted them on design. Even when the project was well advanced, the co-op admitted that it only had partial support from the residents of the area, the majority not being actively involved. It was the support of the council which kept it going.

Unlike other co-ops Calvay did not propose to carry out any major changes in the design or layout of the estate. The proposed development was aimed mainly at carrying out maintenance that was long overdue and correcting some fairly evident design faults that are typical of estates of this type. These modifications consisted mainly of making communal spaces 'manageable and defensible', by apportioning them to particular closes or flats and fencing them and, similarly, dividing and enclosing common balconies and converting ground floor flats into garden flats, to be used by those members with children or special needs. Other repairs were aimed at personalising the otherwise anonymous block, by the addition of new windows, doors, flower boxes, vegetation and landscaping.

More fundamental works have included new roofs, the provision of extra heating and extra protection against condensation, acoustic and thermal insulation, and removing design features known to produce maintenance problems. All these repairs and modifications were required because of insufficient maintenance or misguided design principles and faulty technology used in their construction.

Through the par value co-ops, Glasgow council sought to develop a 'private sector' tool for its public policies. In much the same way housing associations registered with the Housing Corporation set up unregistered subsidiaries to handle private funds. By setting up co-ops which were legally 'private sector' but still containing some element of social ownership, the council sought to get around the situation forced on it by government cuts.

The reduction in the Revenue Support Grant meant that just to carry out day-to-day maintenance the council would have to put up rents. By selling at reduced rates to the co-operative, the repairs could be carried out and the rents kept low, while at the same time the outright sale of the properties to developers could be avoided. Although the DoE must have known this was the case, it could not simply rule out the co-op option, when it had gone to great lengths to defend co-operatives in other areas. On the other hand if the DoE were to allow Glasgow to succeed it might have created a precedent that other local authorities might want to follow. Perhaps the most worrying thing about the community ownership proposal to the Scottish Office was that the co-operatives thus funded would be outside its supervision and control. Like any other private landlords in receipt of council improvement grants, they would remain autonomous and in full ownership of their homes, unless they went bankrupt or defaulted on mortgage payments, or were closed down for gross mismanagement. They might retain some dependence on the council, who set them up in the first place and gave them technical support, but they would not be legally accountable to anyone except the usual statutory authorities.

In view of this it is perhaps easier to understand why the Scottish Office was eager for the co-ops to accept funding and supervision by the Housing Corporation, a suggestion which at first glance appears strangely inconsistent with the government's financial policies, since it involves funding the full cost of the project from public money. But on the other hand it puts the co-ops under the legal control of this body, and severs their link with the local authority.

As a condition of HAG funding, the Housing Corporation retains powers over both the organisation and the property it has funded. It can, for instance, decide to transfer the property from the ownership of the co-operative to the management of another body. Or it can dismiss the management committee of the co-op and appoint one of its choosing. Also, the co-ops lose the possibility of setting their own rents. Under the HAG system the rents must be set at Fair Rent level at least. Thus by agreeing to fund the co-ops through the Housing Corporation the government has ensured ultimate control over their operations and assets.

The similarities to and differences from the Liverpool situation are enlightening. In both cases co-ops have been caught in the crossfire between a local authority and central government. In

Liverpool, co-ops have been used to bludgeon a Labour authority, allowing the government to present itself as a champion of self-management and builder of democracy. In Glasgow, where the local authority supports the co-ops, the government has limited its intervention to blocking and vetoing its proposals, attempting to introduce the Housing Corporation into the equation as perhaps a more reliable instrument of social control.

In the end, the pressures in favour of the par value co-ops have proved too great, and the Scottish Office has allowed the second stage co-ops to go ahead under the auspices of the Glasgow council. Coming so late in the day, and so close to a General Election, it would be difficult not to interpret this as an attempt by the government to cut its political losses on this particular issue, though in the event this didn't prove too successful in Scotland!

8 | Secondary problems in London

In our old Chartist time, it is true, Lancashire working men were
in rags by the thousands; and many of them often lacked food,
but their intelligence was demonstrated wherever you went. You
could see them in groups discussing the doctrine of political
justice . . . or in earnest dispute respecting the teachings of
socialism. Now you will hear well-dressed working men talking,
as they walk with their hands in their pockets, of 'co-ops' and
their shares in them, or in building societies . . . Working men
have ceased to think and want to hear no more thoughtful talk.

This was the view of the Chartist Thomas Cooper in 1870.
Although perhaps overstating the case, there is no doubt that since
the Industrial Revolution co-operatives have been seen by many
as panaceas for the evils of capitalism.

The first building society recorded was very much a 'mutual aid'
association. Founded in Birmingham in 1775, it was set up by the
families of skilled workers to collect savings and provide funds for
house purchase and construction. Success soon changed their very
nature. A Royal Commission, reporting on building societies in
1872, stated:

It appears indeed unquestionable that whilst the smaller,
terminating societies remain very often still under the
management of the working classes, or persons very near to
them in point of station, the larger permanent societies are
almost invariably under the direction of the middle class.

Victorian reformers of various hues, appalled at the exploitation
and inhuman conditions of the time, occasionally propounded co-
operative utopias as practical solutions. Understandably, these
proposals were often based on the reformer's subjective view of

the ideal community, rather than on the hard economic realities of the capitalist system. Thus early co-operative experiments were rarely successful. One which had far-reaching effects was the Rochdale Pioneers' Equitable Society, set up to sell the produce of its weaver-members, which over 100 years ago drew up a list of principles many of which still endure in the co-operative movement as the Rochdale Principles of Co-operation:

1. Open and voluntary membership.
2. Democratic control – one member, one vote.
3. Limited interest on capital.
4. Surplus to be reinvested or distributed equally.
5. Promotion of education.
6. Co-operation with other co-operatives, both nationally and internationally.

The late 19th century and early 20th century saw other attempts at co-operation in the field of low-income housing, such as the Bournville tenants' co-op set up by the Cadburys. But on the whole it was the more financially viable and efficient Victorian housing trusts, with their capital backing and paternalistic attitudes, which managed to consolidate and survive. In his book *Amenity and Urban Planning*, historian and planner David L. Smith noted that:

> All the principal schemes which were implemented between 1853 and 1901 depended on enlightened industrial entrepreneurs who wished to house their own workers in convenient and pleasant surroundings.

Although council housing came to overshadow all 'voluntary' forms of low-income housing provision, the large Victorian housing trusts continued their expansion throughout this period. The Peabody Trust, for instance, by 1880 managed 3,500 dwellings housing 14,600 people. Their scale of operation, and their ability to co-exist with councils by housing 'special needs' groups (such as the old and infirm or immigrants) assured them of continued official support.

It was these organisations that were primarily responsible for setting up the National Federation of Housing Societies in 1936, which to this day remains (as the National Federation of Housing Associations) the main representative body of the voluntary housing sector.

State support

The 1957 Housing Act made it possible for local authorities to provide mortgages for the purchase of properties by housing co-operatives – perhaps the first major attempt to incorporate them into public housing strategy. In Willesden, Reg Freeson, then Leader of the council (and later Minister for Housing), supported a number of co-operatives.

But a really workable model for the formation and funding of housing co-operatives was yet to be developed. Under the 1961 Housing Act money for co-operatives was made available, though apparently the only ones to benefit from these funds were three in south-east London, formed under the auspices of the H. L. Score Housing Society Ltd. Having secured funding for their projects, the three co-ops came together to form the Co-ownership Development Society (CDS) to provide the individual co-ops with the technical services required to carry out their projects. CDS (which later became Co-operative Development Services) was thus the first 'secondary' housing co-operative in Britain, providing development services and management services to 'primary' co-operatives.

The 1964 Housing Act had two major effects on the voluntary housing movement. Firstly it set up the Housing Corporation, a quango of what is now the DoE with overall responsibility for funding from public sources all forms of housing societies. Secondly it created a 'hybrid' form of tenure called 'co-ownership', where a housing society could build or repair property using public loan funds, and then sell it, portion by portion, to individual occupiers in exchange for periodic payments, in a sort of leasing arrangement.

Although initially popular (1,222 co-ownership societies were formed by 1972) the novelty of this hybrid tenure soon wore off, because of high costs and the comparatively high repayments required. Co-ownership was then discouraged as a form of voluntary sector provision, although 'new improved' versions are regularly re-introduced (as, for example, 'shared ownership', 'community leasehold').

The Society for Co-operative Dwellings

A wave of student homelessness brought about by the education cuts of the late 1960s renewed interest in co-operatives. Student Co-operative Dwellings, later to become the Society for Co-operative Dwellings (SCD) was formed in 1968, the year after the University of London Students' Union published a 'Scheme for Student Co-operative Residence in London'. This suggested that purpose-built, shared housing for young single people could be built on the co-operative principle, given the right framework and funding: the Canadian student co-operatives were suggested as a model. SCD was set up to put these principles into practice: its early years are recorded by its founder John Hands – who remained with SCD until the mid 1970s – in his book *Housing Co-operatives*, published by SCD in 1975.

SCD estimated that there were about 5 million persons in Britain beween the ages of 18 and 25. The vast majority of them did not qualify for council housing, nor were they in a position to buy their own homes. The private rented sector was their main source of housing, but at the time it provided less than a million places, some of them notoriously inadequate.

As an alternative, SCD proposed a network of housing co-operatives, made up mainly of young people managing their own purpose-built, communal estates. These estates would include all the necessary social amenities, like communal kitchens, halls and launderettes. Co-ops could range in size from 100 to 500 members – but would be organised in such way as to maximise participation, if necessary by subdividing into sections.

These co-operatives, whose main function would be management, were called 'primary co-operatives' or simply 'primaries'. They would be autonomous, and have clear rules and regulations, ensuring participation by every member. A co-operative education programme would train and inform members so they could be fully involved.

Within this plan, there was a need for a 'professional service' body, known as a 'secondary', which could manage development on behalf of the primaries, and provide them with architectural services and management support. That would be the role of SCD.

Their first co-op was opened in 1974 in Sanford Street on a piece of land offered to them by the London Borough of Lewisham (home to more than one new housing initiative) and part-funded by the Housing Corporation. The balance of funding was provided by Commercial Union Assurance, a private insurance company. It consisted of 14 self-contained houses, each designed for ten single people, and six self-contained bed-sitter flats for couples. Each communal house was on three floors and contained ten bedrooms, each with its own hand basin, two bathrooms, three WCs and a 'farmhouse' kitchen. The houses and flats were furnished, carpeted and centrally heated throughout.

The total cost of the scheme was £377,350, and financial feasibility studies indicated that loans could be repaid, and management, maintenance and services provided to members, all for a weekly rent of £7 (for single people) and £10 (for couples).

SCD went on to set up many more co-ops using a similar framework. The co-op would not be set up by the people needing housing to house themselves. Future residents would not participate in the design or building of their future homes. The scheme would be designed and developed by SCD's professional staff and, prior to completion, suitable residents – briefed as to the nature of the co-op and the role of SCD – would be found to fill it. The founders (who were usually SCD's own executive committee) would then hand over ownership and management to the residents. This later became known as a 'shell co-op'.

State control

But the conditions for promoting and funding housing co-operatives (and indeed, all housing associations), were soon to change dramatically. The 1974 Housing Act introduced the Housing Association Grant system, as the comprehensive method of funding housing association development. The Act also gave the Housing Corporation wide-ranging powers to vet, through the registration process and regular monitorings, those housing associations which would be eligible for public funds. The Corporation also could, if it considered it necessary, intervene or wind up those associations whose performance was found wanting. Although the legislation did not at first include co-operatives, these were brought in as an afterthought, through an amendment in the 1975 Housing Rent and Subsidies Act.

John Hands' view was that the Housing Corporation was not an appropriate body for supervising and funding co-operatives. He considered the Corporation to be a highly centralised and bureaucratic body that favoured a paternalistic approach to housing more appropriate to the Victorian trust than to the housing co-op. As a member of the Campbell Working Party into co-operative housing, (set up by Reg Freeson when Minister for Housing and Construction in 1974, and chaired by Harold Campbell), Hands argued for the creation of a new body, the Co-operative Housing Agency (CHA), to promote and fund housing co-operatives. This would be a promotional and supportive body, and be accountable to co-operatives themselves.

The Working Party did not endorse the proposal of a new body, but did recommend that a section of the Housing Corporation be set up to take on this role. Such an agency was set up with Hands, having left SCD, at its head. A brief 'Golden Age' for housing co-ops followed, where the CHA promoted potential co-ops all over the country, and many were actually registered. But in less than three years, for reasons which were unclear, the CHA was scrapped. Subsequently the Corporation reverted to a more characteristic approach to housing co-ops, treating them as ordinary, albeit eccentric, small housing associations.

In 1975 SCD registered with the Housing Corporation, its name changed to the Society for Co-operative Dwellings. Over the next five years, SCD developed schemes and provided services to over 40 primary co-operatives, as far apart as Brighton, Cambridge and Slough, but mostly in South London. Half of these bodies became registered with the Housing Corporation, but many continued as unregistered co-ops, using short-life properties made available to SCD by local authorities and repaired with the newly introduced Mini-HAG grant or with local authority funding.

By the start of the 1980s, however, SCD was in decline, riddled with external and internal conflicts and suffering chronic financial instability. As Ron Bartholomew, director of the Middlesex Housing Association, wrote at the time:

> Co-ops share the perception of SCD as a shambles of confused objectives which has failed to be a coherent provider of effective services to co-ops.

After five years of registration with the Housing Corporation, SCD had accumulated a deficit of £157,000 in management, and £179,000 in development, which was written off by the DoE. But in 1982/83, after a Corporation monitoring visit, 'financial restructuring' and 'organisational change' of SCD was demanded. At this time SCD was the channel for an average of £6 million per year in grants to housing co-operatives, and had an annual revenue turnover of £600,000.

The crunch came in August 1985, when the Corporation produced a highly critical report of SCD, called *Services to Housing Co-operatives in South and West London*. The document ignored the underlying financial and structural pressures that pushed SCD in a downward spiral. It merely attributed this decline to SCD's 'inadequacies'.

The conclusion of the Report was that: 'The point has been reached where SCD in its present form cannot any longer be considered a proper recipient of public funds.' At a meeting in June 1985, which included representatives of major secondaries throughout the country including SCD, the National Federation of Housing Associations and the recently formed National Federation of Housing Co-operatives, the Housing Corporation recommended the setting up of a group of new secondary agencies to take the place of SCD.

What went wrong?

After discussions with ex-SCD staff, I would suggest the three following factors as the main forces that worked against SCD.

1. *The basic structure*. The idea of a network of autonomous new-build co-ops with SCD at its centre is a highly utopian concept, strongly reminiscent of the ideals of the Garden City movement and Le Corbusier, and probably impossible to implement in practice. They suggest the manipulation of a large number of people around a 'collective' development, in the hopes that they will form communities. Experience (particularly of council estates and New Towns) shows that people do not respond well to this form of 'social engineering', and this resistance will probably be greater among the young and single, who have no particular desire to settle down. 'Sharing' situations, with communal kitchens and dining rooms, are unlikely to accelerate collectivisation. But communal design features not only help lower building costs, they can be justified 'ideologically'.

This drive to create new communities in purpose-built estates led SCD to neglect working with real communities that were already established and which might have provided a more solid human basis for development. Other more pragmatic secondaries – such as Solon Co-operative Housing Services – did not miss this opportunity, helping local neighbourhood groups and squatting organisations to form co-ops, which, being groups with an identity, could take the initiative on questions like design, rather than leaving this up to the secondary. From 1981 onwards SCD attempted to move in this direction, but was discouraged from doing so by the logic of the funding system (which favoured large new-build schemes) and by the Corporation (which would not register local co-ops). Even today, it is probably easier to register a shell co-op by identifying a new-build site, than a co-op based on a local residents' association or a short-life group.

2. *The Housing Association Grant system.* Although at first sight this is a system for providing generous subsidies to all voluntary housing bodies, in practice the HAG system seems geared towards the promotion of large, monopolistic 'social developers', rather than local, accountable housing organisations. The system of development allowances, through which the Corporation effectively pays associations registered with it for each development they carry out is, on the whole, weighted towards large, new-build schemes.

The HAG system also favours those associations practising direct management, particularly on a large scale. Direct management allows associations to build up reserves which they can then use to stabilise their cash flow, funding slumps in the development programme. The inability to weather such slumps was one of SCD's main financial shortcomings.

3. *Housing Corporation control.* In practice the Corporation appears very concerned with the administrative and financial details of co-ops, rather than whether they really allow people to house themselves. It regularly criticises their lack of financial and administrative expertise (in spite of the evident lack of resources made available for training). When co-operatives are found to be 'inadequate' in monitoring, they have attempted to transfer the hard-earned housing of their members into the ownership of large, paternalistic housing associations, insensitive to either the wishes of the residents or the circumstances that might have led up to their poor performance.

If the future of user-control is to be determined by a competition between professional housing associations and lay co-ops to see who is more 'professional', it can only be a foregone conclusion – especially if it is other professionals who are delivering the verdict. If on the other hand the aim is to enable working people to collectively manage their own housing then different criteria must be used.

It could be argued that in its pursuit of administrative excellence, the Corporation has been willing to sacrifice user-control by ordinary people in favour of the continued growth of large housing associations. In International Year of Shelter for the Homeless, it still seems to be supporting the ideals of the Victorian housing trust.

Official consultation

As a first step to the setting up of the new secondaries, the Corporation convened a Steering Group, made up of representatives from the Housing Corporation, NFHA, NFHC, SCD staff and executive council, and the London Borough of Southwark. With the brief of 'establishing a new co-operative agency or agencies to take over from SCD', the Steering Group canvassed a variety of primary co-ops, local authorities and other relevant bodies regarding the proposals. In compiling its recommendations, the Steering Group was also influenced by a study carried out by the Polytechnic of Central London for the Housing Corporation, entitled *A Comparative Study of Secondary Housing Co-operatives*. After carrying out a detailed survey and study of secondary housing organisations in Britain, the research team had put together a series of elements which they felt successful secondaries had in common:

1. They were of manageable scale, versatile, and very accessible to their primaries.
2. They recognised the importance of financial awareness and control, and of continuing co-operative education.
3. In the provision of services they encouraged the independence of their primaries.
4. Their staff and management committees worked closely together towards clear common objectives.
5. Their working agreements with primaries were also simple and straightforward.
6. They allowed their primaries to develop gradually, for instance on the basis of short-life management, rather than expecting them to reach proficiency in a short time with an accelerated development programme.

The Steering Group proposed the creation of three secondaries in London to replace SCD. The main consensus was that the new secondaries should be locally based. In this way they would be more likely to generate confidence and support from local community groups and authorities, which would outweigh any administrative or financial instability produced by their reduced scale.

A west London secondary, the Group suggested, could be based around the work already being carried out by the Middlesex Housing Association. The largest secondary (which eventually became Axle Co-operative Housing Services) should be based in Southwark and Lambeth, where the bulk of SCD's co-ops were, and the third should be based in south-east London, home of more than a dozen SCD co-ops.

The proposals were presented in October 1985 to the Housing Corporation. The Corporation accepted them though it was anxious that the secondaries should see their role less in terms of development and more in terms of becoming managing agents for the primary co-ops. The Corporation said:

> Monitoring has identified the fact that many primary co-operatives have failed to distinguish between 'doing' and 'controlling' their housing activities. Those opting for a self-help approach have often failed to provide an adequate service for their members, which could have been achieved by contracting for services under their control.

With some qualifications, therefore, the Housing Corporation agreed to provide the levels of allocation and grant required to set the secondaries in motion. One of these was CHISEL.

The birth of CHISEL

CHISEL (Co-operative Housing in South-East London) was registered with the Registrar of Friendly Societies in February 1986. One month later it was registered with the Housing Corporation. Its founder members were representatives of Sydenham and Kirkdale Housing Co-ops, two locally-based rehabilitation co-ops registered with the Housing Corporation.

In CHISEL's rules, it was set out that every affiliated primary should be represented on the management committee. Since the Housing Corporation restricted the number of committee members to 15, the membership of the secondary would be limited accordingly. Following registration, CHISEL received requests for affiliation from ten co-operatives, representing a wide range of groups within the community:

- Deptford and Thamesmead Housing Co-ops were SCD shell co-ops. Deptford had become self-managing, Thamesmead had not.
- New Venture was a co-op for elderly people based on a local Age Concern group.
- Tardis and May Day Permanent Housing Co-ops were two short-life co-ops that had registered and were undertaking their first permanent developments. Two Piers Housing Co-op was a small rehabilitation co-op, based in Brighton.
- May Day Short-Life, Blue Moon, Three Boroughs and Lewisham Family Self-Help Association (LFSA), were all unregistered short-life co-ops, some with roots in the squatting movement, and with several years experience of short-life management. LFSA had a sister organisation called Lewisham Family Co-operative Association (LFCA), which was registered with the Housing Corporation, and for whom SCD had developed some permanent rehab properties. As a result of an earlier monitoring visit shortly before SCD's closure, LFCA had been removed from SCD's tutelage, and placed under the wing of Hyde Housing Association, a large direct-management association that also offered services to co-ops.

Sanford Housing Co-op, SCD's flagship, did not affiliate. Nor did Anerley Housing Co-operative in Bromley. As a result of this – and the consequent reduced income from management services – the new budget was already £20,000 lower than had been envisaged by the Steering Group six months earlier. That initial budget had suggested a transition from the provision of development services to that of management services within the first two years. This was in fact proved to be unrealistic since the co-ops preferred to manage themselves rather than buy in management.

In fact, the sole source of income from management services depended on Thamesmead Housing Co-operative, which was not in a position to cope without management support from CHISEL. On the basis of this budget the following staff were employed:
- a co-ordinator/housing management worker, who would have central administrative functions as well as providing management services, primarily to Thamesmead;
- a finance worker, who would provide internal financial control as well as providing training to co-ops on financial matters;
- a full-time and a part-time development worker, who would deal with the bulk of the development programme left by SCD, as well as CHISEL's new programme;

- an education/development worker, who would set up CHISEL's co-op education programme, promote new co-ops, and do some development as well;
- a development/housing management worker, who would be responsible for the short-life programme as well as providing some management services, especially to the short-life co-ops: in May 1986 I was appointed to this post.

With hindsight, and in view of the complex programme left by SCD, CHISEL proved to be under-resourced and understaffed from the start, particularly in the areas of permanent development, co-op education and co-op promotion. One of the cases in which this was particularly evident – and which well demonstrates the problems involved – was at Thamesmead.

Thamesmead – a shell co-op

With most co-ops serviced by CHISEL, the practice was to provide a basic level of advice and support. A much higher level of service was required by Thamesmead Housing Co-operative, which was facing serious financial and managerial problems associated with the way it was set up. This had followed the shell co-op model and the co-op was not cohesive. Its young residents had been referred to the co-op by a variety of local housing agencies, and given tenancies through established SCD procedures.

The estate was quite large, comprising 235 bedspaces, including several disabled units, and some communal facilities. It was originally intended to be a management co-operative, in which SCD would maintain ownership and final responsibility for land and property. One of the reasons for this departure from established SCD practice was given by an SCD internal report:

> There have been considerable difficulties in the establishment of large, new-build shell co-ops as successfully-run co-ops. There has been a high turnover of committee members, difficulty in establishing effectively-run sub-groups and SCD often ends up providing a high level of ongoing housing management direct. SCD's long term involvement seems to be the main safeguard against the risk of such co-ops succumbing to poor administration and lack of proper financial control, and attracting poor monitoring reports from the Corporation.

The demise of SCD cut this initiative short. The group of residents who had been working with SCD as a prospective committee were obliged to take on ownership and management of the estate. This small group was prematurely landed with responsibility for the whole estate, as well as for the considerable liabilities left by SCD. The vast majority of residents, although theoretically members, were in practice either indifferent to the co-op, or regarded it as a 'soft touch'.

Hoping to remedy this situation, the Thamesmead committee entered into a more involved management agreement with CHISEL, in which they paid 20 per cent (instead of the usual 15 per cent) of their management allowances to CHISEL who agreed to provide a direct back-up to Thamesmead staff in dealing with the problems of the co-op. This involved, primarily, appointing and supervising the co-op's own management and finance staff.

When the co-op took over, it had already inherited from SCD rent arrears amounting to £42,000. With support from CHISEL over a period of six months, this figure was reduced to £33,000. A further reduction, however, was unlikely, since many of the debtors had by then left the estate. Thamesmead could thus only continue paying bills and meeting commitments by spending management and maintenance reserves. Obviously, unless this money was replaced, there would be problems in maintaining and equipping the estate in future.

There were other management problems. The co-op had an average of 32 bedspaces empty at any one time, mainly disabled units. Some of this was the result of design problems, the location and condition of the estate making it singularly unattractive to the disabled. On the other hand the Corporation refused to let these units be used by non-disabled people.

After six months of largely fruitless meetings (often at unsocial hours), and countless discussions and training sessions with Thamesmead staff and committee, CHISEL staff felt that they were spending too much time trying to solve the internal problems of this one co-op, to the potential detriment of the services provided to its other members. What's more, it was felt that CHISEL's intervention was not bringing Thamesmead any closer to solving its problems.

CHISEL therefore suggested to Thamesmead committee that

the management agreement between the two bodies should be reduced to the same minimum level to that in operation with other affiliated co-ops. That is, a basic level of advice and education in exchange for an affiliation fee. The responsibility for 'making or breaking' the co-op would then lie where it should be, on the co-op and its residents who could then use the extra money to improve its staffing. But before the co-op could decide on this new arrangement, the decision was made for them. In December 1986 the Housing Corporation monitored Thamesmead Housing Co-operative and gave it a D rating. This meant that it was considered inadequate to continue managing the estate.

This was hardly surprising, given the problems. To ask a small group of residents in an estate of over 200 people to suddenly take over its management – even *without* liabilities of over £40,000 – is to ask a lot of them. Expecting the co-operative to perform adequately under these conditions at a monitoring within six months, as the Housing Corporation did, is optimistic to say the least. In the same vein, it was hardly realistic to have expected the newly formed CHISEL, with its limited staff resources, to assist Thamesmead in this in only six months. The co-op would have had a better chance of success if the liabilities incurred by SCD had been written off, enabling a fresh start.

However now the Housing Corporation recommended that Thamesmead Housing Co-operative be wound up and its assets handed over to Hyde Housing Association, who had earlier been awarded Lewisham Family Housing Co-operative from SCD's stable by the Corporation. This decision has obviously had serious financial implications for CHISEL, which relied on income from affiliation fees and management services from the co-op. For the co-op itself it meant the loss of ownership and control of the estate.

Subsequently, the membership of Thamesmead Housing co-operative voted overwhelmingly to resist the transfer to Hyde – the threat of closure proved a strong unifying factor – and to try to survive as a co-operative. The only basis on which the Corporation was willing to allow it to continue was as a management co-operative in Hyde-owned properties. Thamesmead's committee, feeling unable to go all the way, agreed to this arrangement. Ownership of the estate has now been transferred to Hyde Housing Association.

Problems in practice

By mid-1986 CHISEL had acquired its staff. Some difficulty was encountered filling the posts of development and finance workers, since these tended to be paid above the equal pay rate that CHISEL had agreed. Once staff were in position, the task of taking over the development schemes of the various co-ops from SCD began. This was a complicated, lengthy and expensive process.

With the closure of SCD and redundancy of most of its staff, HACAS (a private consultancy service working closely with the Corporation) had taken over the running of its outstanding schemes. By agreement with CHISEL's Development Group, and as development staff were appointed, CHISEL was handed over the files for each scheme. The private consultant's fees had to be paid by CHISEL from the allowances corresponding to the scheme, which deprived the secondary of income which it desperately needed for 'take-off'. Economies had to be made at every stage, and the small office, eventually located in Catford, was furnished with battered old equipment salvaged from SCD.

In order to distribute decision-making in the most effective manner, the management committee of CHISEL divided itself into the following sub-committees: development; short-life; management/education; finance. But it was not long before major problems were evident in every area of operation.

Development. The main problems here were caused by two proposed shell co-op schemes, for which SCD had purchased sites just before its winding up. In spite of CHISEL's unease with the whole principle of shell co-ops, with its element of 'enforced community', it still had to sort out these schemes since CHISEL's financial viability, and the day-to-day cash flow, depended on securing the corresponding allowances, and on time. Soon after handover to CHISEL these schemes were found to have a host of practical and legal complications. In both cases, delays associated with the winding up of SCD had already outdated work schedules and estimates, requiring complex updating. On scrutiny, both schemes were found to have design faults that would have led to management problems if not corrected. Making these changes, on the other hand, would lead to further delays, and possible financial liabilities to CHISEL. One also presented legal problems that could have resulted in serious financial liabilities to CHISEL, and in the other a property purchased for rehabilitation had nearly collapsed, meaning that the scheme had to be resubmitted as new-build. And so it went on.

To compound difficulties, CHISEL was obliged to form (and register) new co-ops for these schemes. Realising the importance of avoiding 'a co-op in name only' (as Thamesmead was) CHISEL's education worker had to devote a lot of time to identifying and bringing together future residents for both projects. Because of the complexity of the problems involved, the two schemes became a monumental burden on the full-time development worker, to the extent that she felt she was neglecting the smaller development projects of the established affiliated co-ops.

Ironically, CHISEL was allocated, for 1986/87, a further million pounds for the purchase of new sites in Lewisham and Greenwich, which would involve the development of new shell co-ops. These funds were, however, eventually rerouted into buying properties to rehabilitate.

Short-life housing. The problems in short-life development were only slightly less complex. At registration, CHISEL was allocated £50,000 of Mini-HAG funds for the repair of short-life properties in Lewisham and Greenwich for use by co-ops. This represented an allowances income of about £7,000 to CHISEL, and was therefore important to its finances. There was no obvious reason why this Mini-Hag grant should be difficult to spend. There were seven active short-life co-ops in Lewisham affiliated to CHISEL, and the borough had traditionally supported them by providing a steady flow of properties. Greenwich was more of an unknown quantity, never having dealt with co-ops before, but as a sympathetic Labour council was expected to respond to an appeal for short-life property to be used by co-ops. Things did not turn out quite as expected.

Political changes in Lewisham led to a change in policies regarding use of short-life properties. Although during SCD's existence the council had been prepared to supply co-ops with a regular supply of properties, in March 1986 a new reorganised Housing Committee decided to use new properties for the housing of 'priority homeless families' in lieu of bed-and-breakfast. This commendable move had the unforeseen effect of depriving the co-ops, made up primarily of 'non-priority' young single people, of one of their traditional sources of housing. It also brought CHISEL's proposed short-life programme in Lewisham to a premature stop, especially since this decision was coupled with a refusal to grant licence extensions on existing properties held by co-ops until the whole short-life situation was reviewed. This move, damaging to short-life co-ops, was in fact beneficial to large housing associations in the area (Hyde and London and Quadrant) who ran schemes for the housing of homeless families in conjunction with the council.

In Greenwich the situation was similar. Although there were a number of short-life properties available in the area as a result of the proposed Plumstead River Crossing, the council had already entered into an arrangement with Hyde Housing Association for their use for housing homeless families. Apart from this, there were no co-ops in Greenwich in a position to make use of short-life properties.

Eventually, CHISEL identified a group of young people in the area who wanted to form a co-operative and helped them set up Oxleas Housing Co-operative. Negotiations began to try to get them properties, a long process.

CHISEL's delay in getting started on its proposed short-life programme in Lewisham and Greenwich could have had disastrous effects – failure to earn the necessary allowances within the financial year would have thrown the secondary into deficit. Fortunately, a promising short-life scheme turned up in Rochester in Kent, and the Housing Corporation and Greenwich council were prepared to agree to a rerouting of the funds. Six properties owned by Kent County Council were thus repaired for a co-op formed by their occupants. The first CHISEL-promoted co-op is fittingly called 'Great Expectations', referring both to the writer associated with Rochester, and to the conditions that seem to be returning to the area.

Management. The main management problem encountered by CHISEL was another product of the SCD shell co-op approach, as shown with Thamesmead and outlined above. Usually, however, arrangements with most affiliated co-ops were simple and straightforward. Co-ops paid 15 per cent of their management and maintenance allowances to CHISEL, in exchange for a basic level of advice and support. This was usually limited to the odd advice session on management or financial matters as required, telephone advice on matters of urgency, and inclusion in the education programme.

Education. Although CHISEL was in receipt of £10,000 a year in grants towards co-op education, that was not enough for the level of activity required. For a start, it was not enough to fund a full-time worker, so the post had to involve part-time development duties. Since the securing of the necessary development allowances was crucial to CHISEL's cash flow, this tended to take priority over the education function. As well as this, the education worker was also responsible for the formation of the two new shell co-ops that CHISEL had inherited from SCD. Considering that CHISEL had 12 other affiliated co-ops, each one with particular education needs, there was no way that one part-time worker could have done all this justice, in spite of the commitment and willingness to work extra hours that this particular worker had.

If the funding available for staffing was insufficient, even more so was the budget available for for educational aids, publications and staff training, and there was little likelihood of co-ops finding this funding themselves. Not surprisingly, CHISEL's education worker resigned after less than a year, partly because of the pressure and unsocial hours that the job involved.

In the view of CHISEL staff, effective promotion and continued education of co-ops are essential to the success of co-operatives, just as much as the efficient development of their schemes. To ignore this fact inevitably leads to problems and even greater expenditure in future (e.g. Thamesmead). But the income available did not allow them to do this adequately.

Finance. All major problems affecting CHISEL throughout its first months had financial implications, which were only possible to gauge by constantly updating budgets and reviewing feasibilities. The optimistic projections of the Steering Group were not borne out in practice, with the result that the financial limitations on CHISEL's activities were greater than was originally imagined.

This has been particularly true of the income expected from the provision of management services, which was nowhere near what was envisaged. And where such income has been secured, the responsibilities incurred have outweighed the financial benefits. A practical lesson that CHISEL has learnt from its experience with Thamesmead is the danger of embarking on 'open-ended' management agreements with co-operatives in difficulties.

An inevitable consequence of the HAG system for an organisation like CHISEL, that has no management base, is the dependence on income from development allowances. The organisation had to sustain at all times enough development to provide it with regular income so that it could fund all operations without incurring a substantial deficit. Not having any reserves, it could not afford to 'float' such a deficit. Given the difficulties encountered with ex-SCD schemes, maintaining such a balance was precarious to say the least.

Ironically, CHISEL's size has probably allowed it to weather these difficulties with greater ease than a larger organisation, since deficits have tended to remain a manageable size. Nontheless it's been necessary to look round desperately for options that might improve CHISEL's financial viability, such as additional grants and money-making schemes, and to make use of financial buffers like overdraft guarantees from local authorities.

Following on from its first monitoring visit from the Housing Corporation, which responded sympathetically to CHISEL's attempts at viability within an inappropriate framework, CHISEL was earmarked an allocation of nearly £3 million for 1987/88 to work with co-ops in the South-East. Although this does not solve the fundamental problems expressed above, it certainly provides a strong financial basis on which to consolidate the organisation.

Some alternative proposals

On the basis of the first six months' practice, a number of proposals have been considered – which would make it easier for CHISEL to adapt to the disadvantages of the system.

1. *Community-based development.* As a definite move away from shell co-ops, CHISEL has requested an allocation of funds from the Housing Corporation which would allow it to purchase properties in the open market for use by unregistered co-ops under management agreement. This would allow groups that are presently stuck with short-life housing, with the danger of losing properties and having to make their members homeless, to have gradual access to permanent property.

Although there would be initially no need for the co-op to be registered with the Corporation, if this were to take place at any stage then the properties could be transferred to the ownership of the primary. The fact of not having to be initially registered would mean there would be a 'nurturing period' under the wing of the secondary, before having to face the rigours of Housing

Corporation registration.

2. *Initial joint management.* This initial period of joint management prior to registration could also be the basis for a more stable management programme for the secondary, since responsibilities and income would be shared in the first months. But this would be a temporary, nurturing function, and CHISEL would not attempt to 'disable' the primary by keeping hold of management once the primary was registered.

3. *Short-life as a training ground.* In the same vein, short-life housing could continue to be used as the basis for the formation of new co-operatives, by providing groups that want to develop as a community with some properties they can gain experience on, without the risks that the management of permanent property can involve.

4. *Sale of management and education services to co-ops.* Where appropriate, CHISEL could offer co-ops management or maintenance services or packages, such as feasibility studies, financial appraisals or maintenance inspections. But this would be strictly on a cost-basis, avoiding Thamesmead-type arrangements which end up as nearly direct management.

5. *Direct management where appropriate.* The HAG system does not appear to function well where housing organisations do not have access to management income. It might therefore be necessary for CHISEL to look at instances where direct management is appropriate, and the secondary can undertake this function without prejudice to its services to primary co-operatives.

One such area that has been considered is that of 'priority' homeless families, where CHISEL might be able to help local authorities meet their statutory responsibilities by providing short-life alternatives to bed-and-breakfast. This would also allow an opportunity to introduce the families to the benefits of participation.

6. *Education and promotion of unregistered groups.* This is a major area of work that remains unfunded under present arrangements. Since CHISEL's strategy is based on working with and developing these groups, it is imperative that ways of funding this activity are found. In the long term, that involves pressing the Corporation to allow the payment of co-op promotion allowance for work with unregistered and short-life co-ops. For the immediate future, however, CHISEL has secured extra funding from International Year of Shelter for the Homeless for this purpose.

On the basis of these new initiatives, CHISEL feels it could make its operations financially viable in 1987/88. But these initiatives would require flexibility on the part of the Housing Corporation, particularly in allowing its funds to be used for the benefit of unregistered co-ops, something they have been loath to do in the past; and also, in allowing CHISEL to manage properties directly, even though this is a departure from the role that was originally envisaged for it.

Summary

Before the public funding of social housing in this century there was little possibility of co-operative housing organisations surviving at all – they were simply not viable within the competitive, capital-based free-market system. The voluntary housing organisations which did develop during this period, however, were the housing trusts, usually founded on the backs of industrial fortunes. Only in the rare instances where these trusts supported co-operative ventures were co-ops able to survive.

With the advent of the Welfare State and public investment in working class housing, co-operatives at last had a chance, on the basis of subsidy. But the adoption of the paternalist municipal housing model, more in the spirit of the Victorian trust than the co-op, meant that this possibility was curtailed until 1957, when the Housing Act of that year empowered local authorities to make grants available to co-ops, and to transfer assets to them. This led to the formation of the first 'modern' co-ops, in rehab properties purchased from private landlords and in council estates.

In 1964 funding for co-ops and co-ownership societies was made available through the Housing Corporation. Unfortunately this money was used to foster owner-occupation, rather than to popularise co-operative tenure. It did, however, lead to the formation of the first 'secondary' housing co-operative, Co-operative Development Services Ltd (CDS). Then in 1969 SCD launched proposals for a network of new-build primary co-operatives made up of single people, supported by an accountable professional services agency. That agency was to be SCD. In 1973, with the support of Lewisham Council, SCD secured funding from the Housing Corporation and Commercial Union Assurance to build Sanford co-op, a 'flagship' for the movement.

1974 saw the introduction of the HAG funding system and the strengthening of the Housing Corporation's role in the vetting and supervision of housing associations – co-operatives were later included in these arrangements. In 1975, in spite of misgivings about the evident paternalism of this body, SCD registered with the Corporation, and secured an allocation to develop a programme of co-operative development over five years.

During this time, SCD experienced rapid expansion, developing schemes for over 40 co-operatives all over the South of England, including seven large shell co-ops. But simultaneously SCD developed serious financial and administrative problems that, together with its apparent lack of accountability, lost it credibility with its primaries, the Corporation and the movement.

In spite of the Corporation's attempts to pin blame for SCD's decline on its 'managerial inefficiency', the root causes of SCD's problems appear to have been:

1. *SCD's utopian concept.* The ambition of SCD, the creation of a network of self-managing new-build co-operatives made up of single people, was not a practical proposition. Not only did SCD lack the resources to put such a scheme into practice, but residents on the whole did not go along with the 'social engineering' required.

2. *The HAG funding system.* The system of allowances encouraged SCD to be development-led and to aim for wide-spread geographic growth, without providing the necesary promotional and training resources to back up this material development. Also, SCD was unable to use management income and reserves to stabilise its irregular development income, as associations usually do.

3. *The Housing Corporation's intervention.* In its registration criteria, the Corporation showed more concern with the development possibilities of new co-ops, than with the possibilities of achieving self-management. Thus, large shell co-ops that had little chance of becoming communities were encouraged, but not genuine residents' groups or experienced short-life co-ops, which already were communities.

Also, in their approach to monitoring, the Corporation demanded a high level of financial and administrative performance from 'lay' co-ops, whose scale of operation was such that they could not afford to employ such expertise. On the other hand, the Corporation was not prepared to offer extra resources to make these standards achievable.

These factors stimulated in SCD a kind of 'institutional schizophrenia', where it was on the one hand striving to become a powerful and cost-effective large housing association, and on the other, an accountable and responsive secondary co-op. The two models proved incompatible, and the organisation tore itself apart under the pressure of its own contradictions.

In the vacuum that ensued, the Housing Corporation, under pressure from the co-operative movement, proposed new secondary agencies, implementing recommendations that had been made by SCD's staff prior to its demise.

The main evolution from SCD has been the attempt to make the secondaries locally based and accountable to their primaries, and to limit their growth. But although this represents an advance from the grandiose schemes of SCD, it still does not deal with the major anti-co-operative pressures within the housing association framework. Some of these are:

– The institutional encouragement of development-based shell co-ops.
– The discouragement of work with established unregistered co-ops.
– The need to rely on income from some form of direct management to balance the irregularities of development income.
– The inadequacy of resources for co-op promotion and education, particularly for working with unregistered groups.
– The 'disabling' role of the Housing Corporation, in that it has tended to discourage self-management by co-op, and encourage the takeover of these functions by professional associations.

Throughout its first six months CHISEL made great efforts to adapt to these pressures, by finding practical antidotes to the worst effects and by suggesting to the Corporation how those pressures can be ameliorated. The fact that the Corporation was prepared to make concessions to CHISEL must give some cause for optimism, since the Corporation's own policies have played a significant part in the difficulties of secondaries and co-ops. If there is to be any genuine programme for the promotion of user-control of public housing, the Corporation must be prepared to change its practices and the priorities of the funding system, taking on a more 'enabling' role.

If its role does not change, we will not see the realisation of former Housing Minister John Patten's dream, (as quoted in *The Guardian*) of 'people in co-operatives wresting control of their own destinies from unresponsive management', but the continuing nightmare of officially approved housing associations wresting away this control from the co-operatives which have fallen from favour with the Corporation's monitors.

9 | The Colombian context

Conquest and colonisation destroyed the indigenous cultures of the Northern Andes and surrounding areas, just as thoroughly as it destroyed their villages. Some roots remain, and many see in the 'mutual aid' housing practices of today a resurgence of native communalism. Most major cities were founded as administrative and military centres, ports for import and export, or both. Although independence in the 19th century represented a major social and economic change, introducing parliamentary democracy and relatively free trade, the dependent role of the local economies did not change fundamentally from the production of raw materials for consumption in the more developed nations. Whatever industrial and household goods were required were usually imported. Urban population remained a fraction of the total. Bogota's population for example, estimated at 2.3 per cent of the country's total in 1700, had only risen to 3 per cent by 1928.

1930-50

The first significant wave of industrialisation came in the 1930s, as a result of the Great Depression which weakened the economically dominant nations of the West. Export crops lost their international market value, and importers were unable to secure foreign goods. Investment turned to local production, and light consumer industries sprang up or expanded. Several cities now hosted textile, brewing, cement and other manufacturing industries. The landowner-based Conservative Party was ousted from government (after 40 years rule) by a radical Liberal Party, which crystallised the demands of the new industrialists. The new government enacted legislation considered advanced even by today's standards. Working conditions were improved and trade union rights protected. Public housing was initiated. These changes helped to accelerate the growth of the urban areas, doubling Bogota's population between 1938 and 1951.

Housing was not usually a problem for the wealthy. They commissioned local architects (fresh from new architectural schools) to design European- or American-style houses. Cost was not a problem and the necessary materials were either produced or imported. Sometimes foreign architects were commissioned to design and supervise building. For those who could not afford to commission the building of their home, 'off the shelf' houses and apartments for rent were now available from small developers and landlords, who were making a modest start. The ownership of land was initially concentrated in the hands of a few families, but rapidly passed into those of private developers. The fact that labour was cheap and most materials plentiful meant that impressive homes could be built for those who could afford them.

The manual workers, domestic servants and the self-employed, did not, of course, enjoy the same 'freedom to build'. Not being able to afford the services of architects or builders they followed the rural tradition of building their own homes. On land they did not own, or on land where building was restricted by planning laws, using their own labour and traditional materials and techniques (mud, thatch, etc.) they sowed the seeds of today's sprawling 'informal' settlements. From 1928 to 1938 an estimated 2,791 informal dwellings were built in Bogota (out of a total of 9,772). From 1938 to 1950 the figure jumped to an estimated 25,705 dwellings, out of a total of 47,549 built!

The only notable alternative to the informal settlement was the *inquilinato* or rented lodgings in large houses usually in the centre of the city. These houses had once been occupied by wealthier families, but were abandoned in their gradual exodus to the periphery of the city. Now they were subdivided and low-income families crowded into single rooms with few sanitary facilities, while the condition of the buildings deteriorated through lack of maintenance and repair.

During this period of rapid urban growth, a struggle began between the rich and the poor for control of the central areas of the cities. In Bogota, for instance, the municipal authorities attempted to clear a central slum area known as Paseo Bolivar in order to make way for 'residential' development. Resistance was fierce, and although the clearance was eventually carried out, the authorities became less willing to undertake this type of operation again. Eventually, wealthier families abandoned the centre and south of the city, moving to the distant north. Low-income settlements expanded towards the south and east, where the majority of industries was based. Conditions in these settlements were bad, lacking sanitation, services and roads, construction being often deficient and planning non-existent.

Paradoxically, there was little real difference between the so-called formal and informal sectors. Both the rich and the poor found individual solutions to their housing problems, and both built extra housing for rent. The rich (who also made the laws) could afford to build houses that were up to legal, aesthetic and construction standards, but the poor could not.

The main alternative to this model was public housing. In 1928 legislation was passed requiring municipal authorities to invest 2 per cent of their yearly budget on 'workers' housing'. Under these provisions, a municipal housing institute, Caja de Vivienda Popular (Popular Housing Fund), was set up in Bogota and some initiatives undertaken in other cities. This first step in the direction of municipal housing was cut short, under a subsequent Conservative government, by the setting up in 1939 of a national housing authority, Instituto de Credito Territorial (ICT) – the Territorial Housing Institute. This new body aimed at the provision of housing for low-income families – initially only in the rural areas, but in 1942 its powers were extended to the urban areas. ICT had access to subsidised capital, and contracted works to private builders. The properties produced were then sold to individual families by means of low-interest mortgages from ICT. The number of houses built was initially very small, geared towards public employees and 'key' workers. From 1928 to 1950 public housing initiatives were responsible for a total of 3,500 dwellings, as against 57,000 built by the private sector.

A less evident contribution by the State to housing provision at this time was the setting up of the Banco Central Hipotecario (BCH), the Central Mortgage Bank, which collected savings and investments and loaned for building and house purchase at commercial interest rates. The services of this body, however, were confined to higher-income groups, something which has only recently begun to change.

Co-operative housing also made a start around this time,

providing homes for clerical workers and professionals at less than market prices. The Cooperativa de Habitaciones de Medellin (Medellin Co-operative Dwellings), for instance, on the basis of members' savings, and by employing their own development and architectural staff, became one of the city's major housing developers. Co-operative initiatives were rarely evident in lower-income sectors at that time.

1950-1970

The Great Depression and the Second World War had given the country a brief breathing space with respect to international financial forces, but this came to an end in the 1950s. Foreign investment poured into the country and gradually took over 'import substitution'. Financial institutions, banks and corporations gained a dominant role in production. Agriculture was increasingly rationalised (resulting in under-utilisation of land) and mechanised (creating more rural unemployment and migration to the cities). Rates of urbanisation rocketed. Urban population rose from 39 per cent of the total in 1951, to 63 per cent in 1973. Civil war broke out betweeen ruling factions, leading to a populist military government in 1953.

Formal housing production passed almost entirely into the hands of developers, who had access to capital and large areas of land on the periphery of major cities. These developers often built directly, aided by an improved financial structure that made large loans available for development. With growing concentration of capital in the building industry, advanced building systems were introduced for the production of high-rise residential blocks. The majority of developers, however, continued to rely on conventional building methods.

Systems building was also used for the first time in public housing initiatives, in unlikely combination with government-aided self-help efforts. Government housing activity expanded rapidly, in response to political fears and popular pressure. From 1950 to 1954 ICT financed the building of 4,324 dwellings, more than the total it had produced in previous years. The military government was overthrown in 1957, and the new government pledged drastic action to avoid further social strife. From 1950 to 1964 a programme of social reforms was launched, under the banner of the Alliance for Progress. A major example of this drive in the housing field was the building of Ciudad Kennedy, a New Town of more than 80,000 people, covering 450 hectares of land outside Bogota. Half the dwellings were built through aided self-help, and many more through a combination of self-help and private contract. Apart from housing provision, a programme of community development was undertaken, with considerable success. Self-help improvement of informal settlements was also carried out (in Las Colinas, Bogota, for example), as well as in other places throughout the country.

One reform that was to have considerable repercussions in the development of low-cost housing in later years was the creation of a simple framework for community organisation, the Juntas de Accion Communal (JAC) – Committees for Communal Action. These community councils, which could be formed and registered under the 1958 Liberal government's Communal Action legislation, were small, democratically managed organisations, set up by local people with government support to undertake community development projects. They were co-ordinated and often funded by the Ministry of Government which also had a staff of regional promoters who helped set them up and develop projects. Although not intended initially to act as self-build organisations, in years to come many JACs took on this function.

Government housing performance during this time reached an all-time peak, and ICT alone built 84,829 dwellings from 1960 to 1964, more than half through aided self-help schemes. By the 1960s, enthusiasm for this type of initiative waned, particularly towards the end of the Conservative government of Guillermo Leon Valencia. In 1965 only 2,399 dwellings were produced, and although yearly production levels rose to about 10,000 a year in subsequent years, they remained well below earlier levels. The housing deficit continued to grow, and by 1970 it was estimated at over half a million dwellings. The reason given for this cutback was the escalating cost of repaying inflationary foreign loans undertaken to finance these programmes, as well as an implicit political decision to rely more on the private building sector.

The informal sector meanwhile continued to grow, largely unaffected by these reforms. Not all the inhabitants of this sector were self-builders, occupying their own homes. A large proportion of these families rented accommodation, usually a room, from the owners.

1970-1982

After this brief period of reform the government returned to more 'realistic' policies. With the reduction of public investment in development, it decided to stimulate private investment to fill the gap. A system of index linking was introduced, leading to interest rates of as much as 30% p.a. This resulted in a rise in the cost of housing and land, the value of which in Bogota doubled from 1971 to 1977, and to a general rise in construction costs. Incomes did not keep up with these increases, and housing standards were reduced to almost uninhabitable levels.

At the same time government housing programmes relied more on private builders. Instead of aided self-help and similar methods, ICT turned to co-financing with private developers. In this arrangement, ICT would provide funds for construction, the private builder would provide technical services, labour and sometimes land. On completion of the scheme ICT would pay the builder for his contribution, and sell individual dwellings to families from their waiting list by means of subsidised mortgages. This arrangement was no more than a subsidy of commercial building and selling transactions, and in practice did not benefit people with really low incomes.

From 1970 to 1981 ICT production levelled off at about 20,000 dwellings per year, at the same time as the official housing deficit was increasing by at least 28,000 dwellings a year. In 1981 this official housing deficit stood at nearly 800,000 dwellings.

The informal sector continued its unrestrained growth. By 1973 59 per cent of Bogota's population was said to inhabit these areas. Conditions were generally poor – a 1974 survey showed that 617,000 dwellings lacked basic amenities. Having given up pretence of clearing or substituting this sector, State bodies turned their attention towards regulating and controlling it.

The Superintendencia Bancaria – or Superintendency of Banks – a kind of public watchdog over the operations of financial institutions, took a sudden interest in the activities of black market land developers – known as *urbanisadores piratas* (pirate developers) – who operated in the informal areas. These small-time entrepreneurs would sell land which was not theirs, or which was unsuited for housing because of physical or legal restrictions, to low-income families at cut-rate prices. In Colombia, most informal development is a product of these practices. New legislation and planning norms were brought in to define what constituted legal settlements. Self-builders and pirate developers who failed to comply with regulations were 'intervened', and control of illegal developments handed over to a special agency of the ICT for 'legalisation'. In practice, the Agency for Intervened Settlements became a dumping ground for a growing number of settlements (about 200 by 1982), each one a tangle of legal and technical complications which made their legalisation next to impossible. Meanwhile the inhabitants of the settlement would find it difficult to get services, such as electricity, and infrastructure, since legalisation was not complete. In contrast to this, 'non-intervened' settlements were often able to secure these services faster by pressurising the respective service bodies directly.

Some of these settlements achieved a considerable level of popular organisation. In Bogota, a residents' organisation called the Comite Pro-Defensa de los Barrios Orientales (Defence Committee for the Eastern Neighbourhoods) successfully defended communities threatened by a road project for many years. The Central Nacional Provivienda (National Pro-Housing Council) and the Movimiento Civico Nacional (National Civic Movement) also organised the inhabitants of some settlements and provided technical services for improving their conditions. Provivienda in particular has been involved in the formation and support of illegal settelements since the 1940s. A record of these struggles, *La Lucha por la Vivienda in Colombia* (The Struggle for Housing in Colombia) is currently available in print. Recently the organisation has moved away from support of such settlements to the promotion of legal self-build schemes.

Self-build in the 1980s

Partly through the application of official policies aimed at supporting the private sector, by the end of the 1970s living conditions had become so bad that major reforms were once again necessary to avoid more fundamental changes. In 1982 a coalition of several political currents, from traditional Conservatives to Christian Democrats, came together behind Belisario Betancur, a 'populist' Conservative, and ousted the Liberal Party from power. Betancur promised a package of reforms, aimed at creating employ-ment and improving conditions through a programme of public works, which would also encourage commercial and subsidised house-building.

The programme entailed the building of 100,000 dwellings per year, financed from government and private sources. Before 1982, loans from private sources to self-help housing groups were unusual. Most private funding went into commercial building or more expensive housing. But in 1982, in order to ensure that loans would be available, the government decreed that 25 per cent of all investment placed by private financial institutions should be in low-cost housing, and recommended this be done through self-help and co-operative housing organisations. Although these regulations were flouted by most financial institutions (many of whom set up their own firms to build low-cost housing rather loan the money to the groups), they did result in some more private funding being made available. Because these loans carried high index-linked interest rates, groups tried to minimise their use, funding the projects through savings schemes to avoid high financial costs.

The budget of ICT was also doubled, so that at least 36,000 dwellings a year would be built with subsidised funding. The rest would be built with funds loaned on a sliding scale of interest rates. At least half of these would be financially accessible to people with 'legal minimum' incomes or less, who were more than half of the population. The majority of these cheaper dwellings would be produced through self-help, but not in the aided self-help pattern of the 1950s. Instead, loans would be given to non-profit and community housing organisations to develop their own projects. The rest would be built through the traditional co-financing method. With these elements, ICT was able to achieve its ambitious target, and 122,505 dwellings were financed from 1982 to 1984. The BCH financed an additional 40,000 dwellings through non-profit housing organisations.

The combined circumstances of increased housing need and minimal government support stimulated the creation of many non-profit and community housing organisations. By 1982 it was estimated that there were 500 such organisations throughout the country, developing projects for about 80,000 dwellings.

The major problem facing these organisations was acquiring land. If the land was not squatted or bought on the black market (causing future legal problems) or had not been offered by a government body (very unusual), the only option was buy it on the over-inflated open market like any other housing developer – a situation made worse by the accelerated devaluation of the peso.

For example, the value of the peso in relation to sterling had, by 1987, dropped to nearly half of its 1984 value. Through the setting up of savings schemes within the housing groups (something which legislation allowed), enough could be accumulated to make a down payment on a plot of land. This land could then be used as collateral in securing private or government finance to design and build. While this was going on, the future user could continue making regular payments, as well as contributing his own labour to the project, thereby reducing building and financial costs.

Access to subsidised funds remained limited to a few selected organisations. There were a few other ways of raising the money necessary to buy land on the over-inflated open market. Some employers, trade unions and mutual aid societies gave their members small loans with fixed interest rates, but these were usually only enough to cover a down payment on a house. Legislation also allowed for accumulated employees' pensions to be released to finance housing, but this involved a considerable amount of red tape.

Housing organisations

Popular housing organisations in Colombia fall into three main types, according to their origins: First there are housing co-operatives, set up under legislation dating back to the reforms of the 1930s. These have not usually appealed to low-income families, requiring a certain level of income and professional skills to operate successfully. However, some co-operatives have developed much middle-income housing over the years, and provided a model for recent self-build co-operatives for workers.

The most usual type of housing organisation, however, is the already-mentioned Junta de Accion Communal, set up under the 1958 legislation, formed by local people, and co-ordinated and funded by a section of the Ministry of Government called DIGIDEC – the Directorate for Community Integration and Development.

Both these types of housing organisations involve some degree of government supervision and control. This fact has worried many, who feel that this dependence leaves them open to political manipulation, and prevents the organisations from really fighting for their members' interests. For this reason a third type of group has become popular, the independent foundation, association or corporation, with no official links of any sort, but set up on the initiative of trade unions, religious or political groups. Some of them have been set up by housing campaigners and professionals, who see them as a better way of providing low-cost homes than either pressure group politics or government programmes.

Despite their dissimilar origins, many of the organisations had similar methods and objectives, and attempted to use the resources available directly from communities, as well as those accessible through 'legal' channels. In Bogota (and later in other cities) their work was made easier by the introduction of 'minimal planning norms', which allowed for low-income settlements to be built (and receive planning approval) in three stages: site and services; basic living unit; and finished dwelling. Relaxing restrictions in this way allowed self-build groups with even minimal resources to carry out their projects within a legal framework.

The Self-Build Regulations, published by the Superintendencia Bancaria, also helped legitimise the activities of the groups. These defined the requirements of legal self-build projects, and brought them under the official scrutiny. The advantage gained was that groups which met these criteria (which was not difficult) could operate openly as legitimate housing developers.

Although these moves did not represent an integration of organised self-help within official housing policies, it did give these groups a measure of recognition and some space to manoeuvre, allowing for the development of many valuable projects.

A survey carried out in November 1986 by government and university organisations identified 522 housing organisations carrying out projects involving the building of 89,940 homes. The projects were more or less evenly distributed throughout the country but were obviously concentrated in the main urban centres. By 1986 these organisations had handed over approximately 28,595 serviced sites, 2,175 basic dwellings, 8,664 dwellings for gradual development and 1,906 finished dwellings, as well as improving 500 more.

Of the 522 organisations, 133 were JACs, 171 were foundations or associations, 83 were co-operatives and the rest were either registered in another way (e.g. as trade unions or diocesan boards) or not at all.

Recent developments

Given the size and scope of this movement, various attempts have been made to co-ordinate their fragmented activities, and to create a national co-ordinating body that could represent them. A first attempt was made in the 1960s to bring together the co-operatives formed with Alliance for Progress support under a Federation of Housing Co-operatives. But the official change of policy regarding co-ops aborted the attempt. More recently, in July 1982, DIGIDEC organised the First National Congress of Self-Help Housing Organisations, bringing together mainly JACs carrying out self-build projects, and in October 1982, the National Federation of Popular Housing Organisations (Fedevivienda) was formed by several independent housing groups throughout the country. Later that year a government-backed parallel organisation, the Colombian Chamber for Self-Managed Housing (Construyamos), was formed. Apart from these a number of heterogenous regional and national bodies have sprung up, attempting to co-ordinate and represent the different groupings. Thus in 1983, while Fedevivienda had 22 affiliated bodies (mainly large associations), Construyamos was said to have 66 (mainly JACs), a co-operative committee in Cali had 25 affiliates, a federation in Cundinamarca had two dozen more, and so on. This lack of a single co-ordinating body made the possibility of developing a strong movement, able to voice its own demands, more difficult.

Subsequently, the Conservative government of Belisario Betancur declared 1984 the 'Year of the Self Builder', and sponsored a number of joint activities (such as a National Exhibition of Projects) which were instrumental in focusing official and public attention on the movement.

Ironically, one of the main legislative steps taken by the Betancur government with respect to self-help housing groups was a negative one. Towards the middle of 1984 the Superintendencia Bancaria produced 'Regulation 052', a decree which was supposedly aimed at defending the individual members of self-help housing schemes. The regulation made it compulsory for self-help housing organisations to repay individual members who decided to withdraw from projects their total financial investment plus interest, and the nominal value of their self-help input, within a period of four months. This measure, which clearly had individual but not collective interests in mind, could bankrupt small self-help schemes which did not have reserves to pay members who decided to withdraw. A campaign against this measure was launched by Fedevivienda, gaining the support of the other federations, which succeeded in getting the legislation suspended.

In August 1985 Fedevivienda joined with other housing bodies in the country's first 'Unified Housing Congress'. Participants included Construyamos del Valle, a break-away group from the government-sponsored federation, the Movimiento Civico Popular, Provivienda and a national tenants' association. Representatives from 350 organisations attended, representing about 100,000 families. Apart from a first exchange of ideas and experiences, the Congress set up a 'national co-ordinating committee for popular housing' which is still meeting and campaigning jointly.

In 1986 a new Liberal government under Virgilio Barco was elected. The new government has a radical housing policy, which includes new measures to support the self-help housing movement, particularly those schemes aimed at persons with the lowest incomes. Under the slogan of 'creating popular power', the new government has pledged itself to:
– Streamline the legal and technical framework, so that organisations can develop their programmes without bureaucratic obstacles.
– Make subsidised funds available through the Instituto de Credito Territorial and the Banco Central Hipotecario, so that these organisations can successfully complete their programmes.
– Make technical assistance available through SENA (the government's national training organisation), so that these projects have the benefit of professional assistance.

Municipal authorities will also be encouraged to make land and services available for these projects, in order to complete about 90,000 dwellings by 1988.

It is evident that the new government will try to go one better on the limited support given by the earlier Conservative administration. But many things remain unclear. Government house-funding institutions are presently facing bankrupcy, and it is difficult to see where the money to support all these projects is going to come from. It is also difficult to see how land is going to become available, unless strict measures are taken to curb private land speculation. Also, with funding and technical assistance dependent on government bodies (rather than accountable secondary agencies), it is unlikely that these projects will be allowed much autonomy.

Whatever happens it is evident that the self-help housing movement is becoming stronger, and more able to influence government policies and obtain resources. But it is unlikely that this influence will go beyond minor concessions, unless its organisers succeed in uniting the many fragmented local initiatives into a truly representative, autonomous national movement.

Summary

Self-build housing is nothing new in Colombia. It has been the main way in which low-income families have housed themselves since pre-industrial times. The rich have built their own homes, by contracting professional architects and builders. The poor have done it by squatting land, or buying it on the black market and building for themselves, employing skilled help wherever they could afford it. Both groups have also provided housing for rent, to people with more or less their own income level. The difference between the private formal and informal sectors has been more a question of income, rather than any fundamental difference. The rich have more say in the making of laws, and can afford to stay within them. The poor cannot, so their housing is illegal.

The only major change to have taken place in this sector during this century has been the assumption of the financing of middle and upper income housing by financial institutions, and of development by large private builders. This has not been the case with low-income housing, which has continued to rely on the traditional (pre-industrial) self-build principle although gradually introducing industrial materials in place of vernacular technologies.

The State has not intervened to formalise, or to take over funding and development of housing for this sector because it lacks the resources to do so. Instead, it has limited its role to supervising informal development from a distance, only intervening when important principles are at stake. Although some government provision has been evident, at a very low level, this has been little more than a token supply of houses for better-paid workers, and mostly based on subsidising the private building industry and subsidising home purchase. The vast majority of low-income people have continued to rely on informal housing, as owners or tenants, or on the inadequate formal rented sector.

Neither Liberal nor Conservative parties can be wholly identified with public housing provision, since both have expanded it and cut it back at different times, according to their particular political interests at the time. Public housing has only really been pushed forward, by either party, at times of potential social upheaval. First in the 1930s, when it was introduced, then in the 1950s under the Alliance for Progress reforms, and again in this decade. In the 1930s the principle got no further than good intentions. In the 1950s, thanks to a large influx of dollars and aided self-help some progress was made, but abandoned under pressure of the inflationary consequences of these loans. In the 1980s, lacking massive US loans, the government has had to rely increasingly on the contribution of the self-help movement, thereby giving that movement a quasi-governmental character, which has further stimulated its development.

Popular housing organisations represent a sort of advanced informal sector, or, seen from another perspective, an attempt to create 'local-state' welfare organisations to provide for social needs (in the absence of local authority machinery to fulfil this function). They rely on primarily local resources (savings, self-help labour, etc.) to achieve this aim, rather than on public or private capital. Realising the constructive potential of these organisations, the last Conservative government sought to harness them to its 'official' housing drive, by using them as a channel for subsidised and unsubsidised funds, in order to build a large number of houses at a cost-level that private builders would not attempt. But the actual subsidised resources, or for that matter the technical assistance made available for these initiatives, have been minimal (particularly in relation to those going to the private building industry for more expensive housing). Definitive measures to encourage popular housing organisations, such as a realistic fixed budget or the compulsory purchase of speculative development land for use in such projects, have, so far, been avoided.

A new Liberal government has pledged itself to improve matters, by promising a four-year programme of subsidised funding and technical assistance for these organisations, aimed at finishing nearly 90,000 dwellings by 1988. Whether they will deliver the goods remains to be seen.

Lacking any direct political influence on the government (or even an indirect one through a strong trade union movement) housing organisations have so far been unable to gain major concessions from the State. Their strategy for changing this is to form an organised pressure group, with a clear programme of demands, and wide-ranging links with all parties.

The task has been made harder by the dependence of many organisations on political patronage and State funds, which makes them prone to manipulation, and perhaps by the general underestimation of the potential of the movement. However, unless these obstacles are overcome, and some sort of consolidation achieved, it is unlikely that the co-operative movement will ever develop into a primary source of 'popular' housing.

10 | High-tech self-build in Bogota

Founded in the early 16th century by Gonzalo Jiminez de Quesada, Santa Fe de Bogota was for many years the administrative, financial and military centre of the area for colonial Spain. After independence, and the fragmentation of the Nueva Granada vice-royalty, Bogota became the capital of the new Republic of Colombia.

Independence made little difference to the quaint colonial town. It continued to be primarily a political and administrative centre, throughout the internal upheavals that followed. During this time and into the 1800s, its population was a mere 2 per cent of the country's total. In the 19th century some industries became evident, such as porcelain production, chocolate processing, grain milling and brewing. These industries did not develop beyond small-scale manufacture of consumer goods and simple machinery, and imports continued to be the main source of heavier industrial goods, financed by the export of raw materials.

By 1912 Bogota's population had grown to 121,257, still a small proportion of the country's total. In the 1930s Bogota underwent the first wave of industrialisation as a result of the Depression, which weakened the traditional import/export dependency. Its population doubled between 1938 and 1950.

Much of this growth was caused by the migration of rural labourers into the city in search of work, but real employment opportunities were scarce. By 1951 the population of Bogota was 6 per cent of the country's total, and more than 40 per cent of its inhabitants were said to be employed in the service trades and in domestic labour, with consequent low incomes and bad housing conditions. By 1982, with a population of about 5 million (20 per cent of the country's total), it was estimated that 37 per cent of families in Bogota earned less than the minimum legal wage.

157

From the first wave of rapid urbanisation, popular housing concentrated in the centre, south and east of the city, mainly in the form of 'illegal' settlements, self-built by future residents. From 1928 to 1938, out of an estimated 9,772 dwellings built in the city, 2,791 were informal, illegally-built, and lacking in services and infrastructure. From 1938 to 1950 this figure rose to 25,705, out of 47,549 houses built. Not surprisingly by 1973, 59 per cent of all homes in the city were said to be in the informal sector. The growth of these areas was not primarily the result of squatting, but of the illegal sale of non-housing land by black market developers, a practice which was tolerated by the authorities. Conditions in this sector were far from ideal, and a great number of dwellings lacked essential services and infrastructure, and were badly built and overcrowded. The informal sector also provided the bulk of low-income rented housing in the city, in combination with the decaying tenement blocks in the centre of the city. Families were usually packed into a single room, and rents could easily be half a family's regular income.

Government housing initiatives were initially insignificant, and until 1950 only 3,500 dwellings were produced nationally by housing bodies. Under threat of political unrest government provision increased, firstly under the military government of Gustavo Rojas Pinilla. From 1950 to 1954 4,224 dwellings were built in Bogota. With the collapse of the military government and renewed US interest in the area, large dollar loans were made available for mass housing programmes, some of which combined modern systems-building with aided self-help. 14,303 dwellings were built in Bogota by ICT from 1962 to 1964, and Ciudad Kennedy, an 80,000 inhabitant New Town on the outskirts of the city, was successfully initiated.

These untypical programmes were suspended in 1962, under pressure of growing foreign debt. Government building dropped back to its 1930s level, picking up slightly during the 1970s, but generally failing to keep up with the city's growth. From 1972 until 1982 government housing production levelled off at about 20,000 dwellings per annum at the same time as Bogota's housing deficit increased by about 18,000 dwellings per annum, reaching an estimated 350,000 in 1982.

It is not surprising that more effective alternatives were looked for, and found. The 1982 government of Belisario Betancur gave those new initiatives the opportunity to prove and consolidate themselves.

Origins of AVP

The Simon Bolivar Association for Popular Housing (AVP) began as an informal discussion group made up of some housing professionals (with public and private experience), radical priests, and community activists. They met under the auspices of a local information centre called the Centre for Popular Education and Investigation (CINEP), supported by radical church groups, and considered subversive by more reactionary sectors.

Unwilling to merely discuss social issues, the 'think tank' jointly developed a proposal for a pilot housing programme, which would begin to answer the problems of the urban poor. This project, and the background to it, was eventually presented in a very lucid paper in 1982. The members of the group identified the failure of both private and state sectors in providing housing and other basic social services for those most in need. The high cost of commercial housing could not be met by the low-paid or unemployed, and the low level of public funds available for subsidised housing, coupled with the inadequacy of the institutions handling these funds, made this provision ineffective.

On the other hand, they noted the spontaneous self-help efforts which accounted for a fair amount of the country's low-cost housing. These settlements, although far from adequate (or for that matter economic), demonstrated that there was potential both for funding and self-building housing and community facilities, if the resources available to low-income communities were effectively managed.

They suggested that a project could be developed where a team of committed professionals co-operated with a low-income community in order to carry out a substantial housing development that could also become the basis for other projects and to meet other community needs, such as health, education and employment. The community could provide the money, either directly (from savings, or using a percentage of earnings) or through its mortgage capacity. It could also provide the labour power to make the project work. The professionals, on the other hand, could design the project, establish the administrative and financial framework in which the project could develop, and help the community organise itself. They could also deal with State and financial bodies and take care of the paperwork. When the housing was completed and the other projects off the ground, the professionals could pull out, leaving the community to manage itself.

The think tank based its proposals on a few prior experiences: the Asociacion de Destechados Camilo Torres (The Camilo Torres Association for the Homeless) in Pereira, which since 1979 had been developing a project involving 200 families; the long-established Cooperativa Medica (Medics' Co-operative) del Valle, providing housing for middle-income professionals; as was the Asociacion de Educadores (Teachers' Association) del Quindio, a trade union organisation.

It is notable in the AVP experience that the proposal was discussed, researched and carefully developed before any attempt was made to put it into practice. From those initial principles, agreed between 1980-1982, the present structures, methods and objectives have evolved. The fact that those founding principles were solid has allowed the project to develop on course to this day.

The professional team

In 1981 the Association was registered, with a management committee of seven, and no members. In 1982, permission was obtained from the Superintendencia Bancaria to develop the first part of the project – 500 dwellings. In order to proceed, a technical team had to be found which could take the project through its initial stages. Eventually seven people were selected – an administrator, an accountant, a lawyer and three architects, under the supervision of an architect/director. They were appointed on a part-time basis. The team, making use of consultants and appointing casual clerical staff to help with sales, paperwork and preliminary sketches, ran the Association for the first months under the supervision of the management committee.

As money started to come in, from payments made by affiliated members, staff employment could be regularised. But before this could happen, the team had to put together a saleable package: identifying land, presenting preliminary designs for dwellings and working out payments required from potential members. Without this, no one could be reasonably expected to invest their life savings on the scheme. Happily, the team did its work well, and by the end of 1982 the package was ready for presentation.

The package

Land. After identifying and investigating various parts of the city where land could be obtained at desired costs, the team opted for a 46-hectare *hacienda* (farm) that was on the market, on the north-western periphery of the city. The land was big enough to permit a large housing development (about 5,000 dwellings) and although it had no services these could be acquired. Access was good, and would improve in the future, thanks to a planned highway development. The land was flat, and it bordered on a neglected natural conservation area, giving it ecological potential.

Urban design. The urban layout was designed with a view to facilitating access to dwellings and communal facilities. From a nearby highway a semi-circular primary road joined several secondary radial roads that covered all sections of the development. Off these secondary roads, car parks were regularly placed, with pedestrian access roads to all buildings and communal facilities. All parts of the plot were more or less equally accessible. Communal facilities, medical centres, schools, recreational facilities and green areas were also strategically placed.

Architectural design. The initial criterion in design was to minimise the individual area allotted to each dwelling (but to not less than nine square metres per person), and to maximise space for communal facilities. From an early stage, the Association opted for five-storey walk-ups, deciding they were the most appropriate for the scheme, particularly for financial reasons. Since planning regulations required that buildings over five storeys have lifts, anything taller would become uneconomic.

Construction method. Due to what had already been decided, the method used had to be appropriate to massive housing schemes. From the start, AVP discarded the idea of traditional self-build, with each family building its own home using traditional methods. It felt this would lead to slow work and poor performance. Therefore, it decided to look at medium and high technology building systems, as well as more conventional building methods. In the end, it commissioned a feasibility study from a prestigious building consultant. The study covered the range of apparently suitable technologies, from pre-fabrication, through structural blockwork, to 'shuttering' systems' that allowed walls and floors to be cast on site, as well as heavier 'on site' moulding systems.

The study took into consideration the very high costs of importation, as well as the Association's need to rely on self-help labour, which meant the system had to be suitable for use by unskilled and semi-skilled workers without great quantities of additional machinery. The possibility of making a substantial initial investment in a good industrial system was not ruled out, since it was likely that a community enterprise could be developed subsequently on the basis of building to contract.

Eventually, the decision was made to use the Con-Tech 'shuttering' system, which required considerable initial investment but, once bought, would be suited to the Association's requirements and allow for the development of a community building enterprise in the future.

Cost

The package had a price, and this price had to be within the means of future users. After considering every way of lowering costs without reducing conditions below an agreed standard, the Association decided to accept onto the scheme only families with a monthly income of at least 25,000 pesos (then about twice the legal minimum wage). This excluded most of the city's population, but even so would reach a lower income level than most of the government's programmes (which were usually aimed at people earning more than 35,000 pesos per month). This income limit was calculated on the basis of the minimum income needed to sustain a private mortgage, to pay for the part of the project that would not be directly funded by savings.

The final price of a finished dwelling (three bedrooms, kitchen and dining room – 57 square metres in total) was in 1986 quoted at 26,000 pesos per square metre – giving a total equivalent cost then of about £4,500 per flat. In contrast, a nearby 'low-cost' private housing project was selling at 42,000 pesos per square meter. Most commercial development in Bogota is well above this figure.

It was initially suggested that each member should pay 20 per cent of the total cost of the dwelling over the first two years of the project, from savings and small regular payments. A further

30 per cent could then be secured in the form of low-interest loans from employers and union organisations, pensions and employees' bonuses. This would leave only 50 per cent of the cost of the project to be loaned from a Corporacion de Ahorro y Vivienda (CAV) – Corporation for Saving and Housing, the equivalent of a building society.

By 1984, the Association had been forced to modify this scheme, since the low-interest loans and pensions were not forthcoming to the extent hoped. Members were therefore expected to finance 25 per cent of the cost of the project directly, the rest being met from private mortgage funding. The actual methods of payment of this directly-funded portion was agreed by the member and the Association, on the basis of a recommended schedule of payments. In spite of these facilities, arrears were high and by 1984 members owed 11 million pesos in direct payments to the association.

In 1984, with nearly 2,000 families registered and contributing towards the scheme, AVP secured loan approval for 75 per cent of the cost of the project from two building societies (CAVs), both connected with progressive church organisations.

Selling it

The task of getting those first 2,000 families to invest their life savings into an apparently utopian scheme without seeing a single house first was no easy matter. It is perhaps an indication of the desperate housing need that most people in Colombia face that the task succeeded. Publicising the project was tackled methodically, on the basis of lists of major firms, trade unions and mass organisations in the city who were likely to be in touch with people of this income level. These institutions were then visited one by one, and the scheme was explained to union officials, personnel officers and large meetings of trade unionists. This often led to long negotiations, which sometimes resulted in block-bookings by these institutions. In addition to this direct canvassing, adverts were placed in local press and on the radio, and people invited to visit the Association offices and find out more about the scheme. A model of a typical walk-up block was available for inspection, as well as drawings and flat layouts. Eventually, the project became so well known there was no further need to advertise it and a steady stream of enquiries became normal.

Self-help organisation

The intention of the Association was to create an efficient members' workforce which could make a real contribution to lowering the cost of housing. Every member was expected to devote a number of days to working, either on site or at the Association's offices. Initially, 156 working days were required of each family group as a minimum, but by 1984 it had been lowered to 90 days. The value of this work for the future dweller amounted to between 7 per cent and 12 per cent of the cost of the dwelling, and more if the member had particular skills which were required by the Association, or worked for more days.

The work schedule was carefully structured by the Association, and carried out on the basis of regulations agreed with members' representatives and scrupulously adhered to. Workers were organised into brigades, supervised by semi-skilled brigade leaders and in turn co-ordinated by a site manager. The site manager also carried out quality control and the AVP architect would make regular site inspections. Careful control was kept of who worked what hours, of equipment loaned out and materials used. Paid labour was not accepted in lieu of members' own work.

Self-build shifts, apart from reducing costs, were intended to create solidarity within the community and so were usually happy, hard-working affairs. A restaurant was set up by members to cater for workers on site. A creche was put into operation for the children of self-builders and a first-aid centre was also on daily call.

Community development projects

Four other major projects were simultaneously being developed by the Association. These were:
Health. The eventual aim was to provide comprehensive medical cover for all members of the Association (and surrounding areas). Initially, a small health centre was provided, and a regular surgery served members at nominal cost. It was expected to develop into a fully-fledged clinic, providing everything from dental treatment to minor surgery, and with the back-up of a nearby hospital. This was later complemented by a programme of preventative medicine and nutrition, which also trained community health promotors to monitor health needs.
Education. Again, a range of services was to be provided, from

nursery to secondary schooling, and even further education courses for adults on a variety of subjects. These included social sciences, arts, physical education and health studies, as well as technical courses on electronics and (of course) building.

Ecology. Starting out with the protection and improvement of the local environment (through re-afforestation and measures against local pollution), the group intended eventually to campaign on environmental issues affecting the whole city and the country.

Community industry. Starting with the metalwork, carpentry and building materials workshop, the Association intended to develop community-based industries, to provide employment and raise the general level of income. Investigations were underway to identify other suitable low-technology industries which could be developed by the Association. It is interesting to note that the Association was looking to the Mondragon industrial co-operatives in northern Spain as an model of what they wanted.

These four projects were allocated funds and human resources by the Association, in consultation with members' committees set up to organise each one of them. The self-help labour requirement did not only apply to the building work. Nurses and doctors therefore could work their self-help shifts at the local health centre, agronomists plant trees, ecologists investigate pollution, carpenters and metalworkers work at the Association's workshops.

There were also other active members' committees which did not have the status or funding of community projects but nonetheless contributed to members' enjoyment and integration. They were the arts committee, in charge of exhibitions and concerts, and the sports committee.

Community organisation

AVP had an apparently complex structure, due to its large membership and the wide range of activities it carried out in addition to housing. It is was almost two parallel structures, working in tandem. The first was the 'professional' structure, made up of management committee and staff. The committee was made up of the priests, professionals and community activists who set up the project, and who had ultimate liability for all the Association's operations. Then there was the staff, appointed by that management committee, divided up into various departments – development, financial, legal and community organisation being the main ones. Staff organisation was hierarchical, but decisions were taken on a fairly collective basis.

The other was the 'user' structure, organised on a pyramidal basis. At the base were the area committees (one for every 500 members) and the project committees which represented the various areas of activity (education, health, employment.) Each one of these committees elected representatives to form part of a central co-ordinating committee which was the overall represent-ative body of the membership. Each project committee was charged with developing its own specialist area, and for that purpose received staff back-up and a budget from the Association, as agreed with the central co-ordinating committee.

Although this structure allowed members to participate in a variety of projects connected with the development of the community, it fell short of giving them control of the development process. In practice, technical and financial decisions were taken by the paid staff, and rubber-stamped by the management committee.

It could be said that AVP was trying to perform a dual role. On the one hand it was a secondary development agency, providing professional services to an organised community of users. But on the other hand, AVP also attempted to represent that community through its own structure, a task not always compatible with its professional interests. This amalgamation between the 'primary' role of user-representation and the 'secondary' role of providing professional services is frequently found in Colombia, and can perhaps be explained by the fact that current self-build legislation does not promote the creation of secondary agencies. But there is evidence that many of these organisations are evolving into secondaries. AVP for instance, intends to hand over management of the estate to a user-organisation (probably a JAC) as the building is completed. The Association thus envisages performing more of a secondary role in future developments.

Office organisation

With the growing workload, the full-time staff at AVP expanded. The community organisation section dealt with the community development projects, direct payment arrears, organisation of self-build, and so on. The financial section kept financial records, received payments and serviced loans. The legal department dealt with contracts and loan agreements as well as individual members' legal problems. In spite of a computer, AVP had to expand both office size and staff numbers, from an initial seven, to about 30 paid staff, with self-help back-up from members.

Problems

Several major problems arose in the development of the scheme, some internal, others external. From the start AVP attempted to provide a democratic structure for participation by future users. At the same time it was implementing, step by step, a large and complex housing development. Given the rapid rise in membership and the almost unavoidable obstacles it has encountered, it is understandable that some members would question the Association's management of the scheme. Some have just withdrawn, and have been reimbursed. Others have preferred to. 'make a stand', using the framework provided by the Association, either to put forward their ideas as to how the project should be run, or to suggest changes in the present management.

AVP has found such internal dissidence difficult to handle, given the complexities of the building project and the shortage of staff time to deal with these situations. The dissidents have been so far unable to become a significant proportion of the membership, but they have managed to make trouble. They went as far as to try to squat project land (with the avowed intention of 'building their own houses') and to report AVP to the Superintendencia Bancaria for supposed mismanagement. Eventually, the most extreme dissidents were expelled from the project, but not without causing considerable damage through the publicity given to their activities.

On at least two occasions, the continuation of the project has been threatened by the action of State bodies. First, in November 1983, after the final plans had been approved by the municipal planning office, the water authority informed them that a large chunk of the project was outside their 'services perimeter', so they would not be able to supply it. Apparently the trouble was that the water authority used a different perimeter boundary from the planning authority. After a heated campaign involving occupation of the water authority offices by members of AVP, pickets outside the Presidential Palace and many press articles and letters, the water authority backed down and accepted the planning authority's boundary.

In June 1984, partly in response to the complaints of dissident AVP members, the Superintendencia Bancaria issued new regulations, requiring self-build projects to return to members who withdrew all the contributions paid to date, plus interest at commercial rates, plus a nominal payment for the self-build work they had carried out. Since most organisations of this type worked on a hand-to-mouth basis, it was unlikely that they could meet this requirement without putting themselves in danger of bankruptcy, especially if several withdrawals took place at once. After another campaign, co-ordinated by Fedevivienda, the regulation was 'temporarily suspended'.

Summary

At the beginning of 1985, AVP handed over the first 140 apartments, with a further seven blocks due to be finished by May of that year. A recent newspaper report in *El Tiempo*, the leading daily newspaper, called this 'pilot project' – as they termed the first phase, involving 2,000 apartments and nearing completion – a resounding success.

It is a striking example of how a large self-help housing project can be initiated by a small core of professionals, basing themselves on the financial and labour input of a low-income community. Using this principle AVP has successfully begun a relatively large project, without any government support.

Finance has come from two sources: savings, earnings and other funds available to future residents (which covered about 25 per cent of costs); and private loan funds (which financed the remaining 75 per cent). AVP has tried to maximise direct funding to reduce financial costs.

Land was purchased on the open market after careful investigation, and the size of the project allowed a considerable initial accumulation of capital (from members), which in turn permitted the purchase of a considerable piece of land. This initial investment secured building land for future stages of the project, and also protected savings from inflation.

The project only depended on local authorities for services (although some internal drains and roads would be built by the

Association). This dependence has not been without problems, both in delayed approvals, and in a potentially disastrous dispute over boundaries. But, apart from encouraging a closer link with the service boards, there is little that could be done to improve this situation.

The aim of the project was to provide housing (in the broadest sense) to 5,000 families, as well as a range of community facilities and social services. The key to achieving this has been the organisation of future residents, and the use, as far as possible, of their own energy and resources. To make this possible a democratic structure has been encouraged within the Association, with elected representatives of members participating in, and actually running, many aspects of the project.

But whereas members have *controlled* the various community development projects and activities relating to the community, they have only *participated* in the implementation of the housing development programme, which had been previously determined by the technical team and the management committee. This was partly due to the sequence in which the project was initiated, partly to the commercial framework in which it was developed (the need to sell a product), and partly to the fact that the importance of such control was never raised.

Once the initial project had been determined by the technical team, future residents were found by methodical approaches to mass organisations, and by public advertising. These future residents were formed into a community by integrating them within the structure of the Association, making every future resident a member, enabling them to participate in general policy meetings and to be elected onto committees in charge of various social activities. With hindsight, the question is whether this was the best way of integrating them.

On the one hand the community had to organise itself and needed a framework to do it in; on the other hand, the development process had to be efficiently carried on by a technical team, with the collaboration of the community. Another answer would have been to form a separate community organisation from the start, and avoid dangerous struggles for control of the development body in mid-project. But it was important to ensure that the development body continued to be accountable to the community which was financing it. Although no definite decision has been taken on this by AVP, it has been suggested that finished dwellings be handed over to a separate members' organisation (probably a JAC) for management and maintenance. Since all the properties are owner-occupied, each resident will be asked to pay an additional monthly fee to the user-organisation for this purpose.

Although the technical team has been excellent in its handling of resources in the project (a product of their unbiased initial selection), they have on the whole based development decisions on abstract technical and financial considerations, rather than on any form of consultation with future users. The choice of building types, of dwelling design, of construction technology, the self-build organisation, are all based on 'sound' professional decisions, rather than being the preferences of future residents. Time will tell whether this approach will not run into the same social problems that government bodies have found with similar mass housing projects.

One very positive aspect of the AVP project has been that it has not stopped at housing, but developed a range of social services and community facilities, giving members the opportunity to put non-housing skills to use. One could argue that this job should be performed by municipal authorities, and that AVP is letting them off the hook. But municipal authorities in Colombia are not used to this role, and have few resources available to them to perform the few services they are responsible for. A better alternative would be for municipal authorities and central government to work with organisations like AVP, giving them access to public resources and integrating them into their local plans. This would probably allow them to reach a larger section of people, and particularly those with the lowest incomes.

11 | Intermediate technology in Manizales

Manizales stands on a long narrow Andean ridge, 2,000 metres above sea-level, in the heart of the undulating, fertile 'golden coffee triangle' in the south west of Colombia. Founded in 1848 by immigrants from nearby Medellin, by 1850 it had a mere 2,789 inhabitants (mainly small farmers looking after a few head of cattle), and no factories or schools.

With the boom in the coffee trade of the late 19th century, Manizales acquired importance as a trade centre, from where coffee could be shipped to the outside world, and imported machinery and manufactured goods obtained. By 1905 the population had risen to 24,700, and by 1918 to 43,203. Its strategic location between the main economic centres of the fertile south-west determined its primary function: to transmit goods and imports, with a secondary activity of exporting gold, hides and coffee.

In 1921 Manizales was given a boost by the construction of a massive cable car which connected it with Honda, a principal river port with access to the Caribbean. In the late 1920s this was replaced by a direct railway link with the coast.

Informal popular housing development was evident in Manizales around this time. Land surrounding a new road to the north was occupied by squatters, who formed the Sierra Morena settlement. In order to cope with the unusual steepness of the terrain, families fell back on a traditional building method, using bamboo. There was no shortage of the basic material, thanks to the fertile soil, so tall pier-frames were built, and infilled with bamboo bark and mud (*bahareque*). Over the years the settlement withstood heavy rains and earthquakes (where supposedly solid buildings collapsed), and succeeded in obtaining services and roads from the municipal authorities. The Sierra Morena remains one of Manizales' most unusual neighbourhoods, a monument to traditional skills and informal methods.

Technologies like these never caught on with the formal sector, probably due to difficulties in standardising them for commercial use. Two major fires in the city encouraged the belief that they were unsound (much as the Great Fire of London did for timber frame), and they were eventually discarded in favour of more conventional technologies – until their recent re-discovery by researchers.

Not surprisingly, one of the first industries to come to the city was the production of cement, followed by agricultural machinery, textiles and thread, leather goods and beer. Fiscal incentives to move from larger cities ensured further industrial development. By 1960 the population had risen to 177,000 and by 1970 it was estimated at 285,000. The general decline of opportunities in agriculture, caused by shrinking markets for traditional cash crops and growing mechanisation, have, in Manizales as elsewhere, accelerated migration from surrounding rural areas. But, like its larger counterparts, the city offered neither work nor welfare provisions for the new arrivals. They, like the less fortunate natives of the town, were forced to help themselves to survive.

Protecho

As a result of these pressures a militant housing organisation was formed in 1970. It was called Protecho and was made up of activists and large numbers of low-income people in need of housing. The first actions of the group were confined to pressure group politics: meetings were held to discuss the housing shortage, delegations were sent to argue its case with local authorities and the government housing institute, demonstrations were held at their offices, and so on. When it was evident these tactics were not going to produce any major change, an occupation of vacant land belonging to the Instituto de Credito Territorial was carried out by activists and homeless families. The confrontation, however, took place when they attempted to secure services for the settlement (called Camilo Torres – after the revolutionary priest). Only after a vigorous and sometimes violent campaign did the organisation succeed in obtaining infrastructure and services from the authorities.

Having achieved the consolidation of the settlement, organisation and activity declined. Many of the original activists sold rights to their dwellings and left. No further community development projects were undertaken, and the settlement reverted to being just another low-income neighbourhood. The area has subsequently become the electoral bastion of a local politician from one of the traditional parties and apparently retains very few lessons from its dynamic origins.

From Protecho to Fundemos

Many of the founders of what would become Fundemos – the Foundation for the Integral Development of Manizales and Caldas – were involved to some extent in the Protecho experience. Some of them were students at local universities who gave technical support to the settlement. Others were interested in the social and political possibilities of the movement. All of them were disappointed and made wiser by the limited achievements of the experience. By 1980, a small group had started meeting, with the object of setting up a new association, based on the lessons of Protecho.

They were now sceptical of both pressure group politics – because a lot of pressure was required for very limited gains – and of the wisdom of starting out with forcible land occupations. Much of the group's energy in both cases seemed to be absorbed in essentially unproductive activities – such as conflict with the authorities – rather than the job of building their community. The founders of the new group did not for one moment believe that conflict with the authorities was unavoidable at some stage, but they felt that conflict was being unnecessarily generated through lack of use of official channels, lack of technical expertise and an overall lack of clarity on the part of the organisers as to what exactly they were trying to achieve.

They set out therefore to think out and design a new project, which would make use of whatever formal facilities there were for developing the community, as well as of the resources and energy of the community itself.

Integral community development

One of the principal faults that the founders saw in the Protecho experience was the lack of any real development of the community. People had been organised, and their resources used to provide them with a home. But after several years only a very basic dwelling had been achieved. No other needs had been met by the community organisation.

The new organisation should not take this one-sided view, they thought. It should aim at developing its members as individuals by educating them on a whole range of topics. It should also be developing the community's ability to fill its other needs apart from housing, providing adequate health facilities, employment possibilities and a clean environment.

This they called 'integral community development', and it became the primary objective of the organisation.

Composition

The founders accepted from the start that a partnership between two separate groups was required to create an effective organisation. One was the community itself. In this case it would be primarily working families, employed on low wages or under-employed in some form of service trade, not able to secure a mortgage to buy their own houses, and unlikely to be favoured for a government dwelling. This community had resources – savings, a proportion of members' earnings which could be set aside, their capacity to self-build – which could be used as the basis for providing for their needs.

The other was the team of professionals who had come together through the Foundation and who could lend their skills to ensure the community's resources were put to the best possible use, and could help them make use of official channels and formal resources. This group was also aiming to fill their need, but this was of a slightly different nature – the need to use their skills in a rational, socially relevant manner, in conditions where they could have a modicum of job satisfaction.

The structure and activities of Fundemos were designed to allow for both.

Formation

Fundemos was set up in August 1981. It was a non-profit organisation, empowered to carry out housing, health, education and ecological projects. Its 17 founding members were mainly young professionals – doctors, engineers, architects, solicitors – sharing the same radical background. Its founding capital was a mere £2,000.

Fundemos scrupulously carried out all the legal requirements that its future activities called for – registration with the Superintendencia Bancaria, with the Chamber of Commerce, etc. – and moved into a small rented office in the centre of the city. From there, Fundemos began developing its parallel, but inter-related, activities in the areas of housing, production of building materials, health, education and ecology.

Groundwork

The Fundemos housing project began in earnest in 1981, after a workshop for the production of building materials had been secured and the first offices taken up. Advertisements were placed in the local press and on radio to let people know about the Foundation and its objectives, and asking potential self-builders to contact them. On this basis, and through personal and institutional contacts, the first 200 families put themselves down for the project.

The founders opted for a small scheme to begin with. This was partly because of their relative inexperience in this type of project. They felt that if they tried it on a small scale they were less likely to make serious mistakes and could learn for future schemes. Also, they wanted a quick start.

A small technical team was set up to meet with the future users and decide on what kind of scheme to carry out. This involved visits to two associations developing similar projects. One was the Asociacion de Destechados Camilo Torres in Pereira. The other was AVP in Bogota. Something was learnt from both.

The Destechados project was attractive technically. It used a conventional construction technology (reinforced concrete, cement block infill) which Fundemos felt it could handle. Destechados manufactured its own concrete blocks and other construction elements. Self-builders could use this technology without much difficulty. AVP, on the other hand, seemed to have the organisational model Fundemos was looking for. It sought to combine the skills and co-ordination of a professional team with the resources and labour of a democratically organised community. It used whatever formal facilities and official channels were available.

The study of these two projects gave the team and the future residents a fairly clear picture of what they wanted to create.

The project

In May 1982 the technical team and the community agreed on a proposal that was to form the basis of the housing project. They first defined the objectives of the project thus:
– To allow people on low incomes to have access to adequate housing by eliminating profit and achieving economies, through use of self-finance, self-build and direct production of building materials.
– To complement this project with involvement by future users in other projects being developed by the Foundation, in health, education and ecology, in order to stimulate integrated community development.
– To develop within the housing project (as well as in the other projects) the principle of self-management by the community of its housing and social services.
– To bring together resources available to communities with 'official' resources, in order to promote pilot projects which could be used as models by future organisations.

The project was to be developed within the definitions and regulations set out by the Superintendencia Bancaria, the government body charged with the supervision of such projects.

The community (the future users) would provide funding from savings and regular payments, and their ability to self-build. The Foundation (the technical team and management committee) would provide technical direction for the project, organise the use of resources including self-building, identify appropriate technologies and materials and arrange for the direct production of building materials. It would also promote the complementary health, education and training programmes.

An important element in the proposal was the setting up and development of a building materials production workshop, as a parallel community enterprise. This workshop was important as it would reduce the extra costs which would be generated by commercial purchase. The workshop could investigate and develop production of building materials and building systems which might be more appropriate than those conventionally used, and provide a source of employment and income in the future.

A certain ambiguity in who actually controlled what was apparent in the initial proposal and in the administrative structure suggested for it. On the one hand, future users were democratically organised and could elect a members' committee to supervise the project. On the other, the Fundemos Management Committee appointed a project co-ordinator and a technical team to carry out the development itself. The co-ordinator and team were not directly accountable to the members' committee, but worked closely in consultation with it, particularly regarding payment of members' dues and self-help labour input. In practice, two organisations were operating and developing: the technical team – a sort of professional collective – and the self-managed community. A clear understanding of this from the start might have helped a clearer definition of roles and responsibilities, and avoided conflicts which arose later between the two parties.

Land

The first few months of the project's life were taken up with the search for a suitable plot of land on which to build. All leads were followed up for both private and government-owned land, and many sites were visited. A typical land inspection would involve a convoy of vehicles, containing not only the technical team, but a number of keen members and their families, all determined to have a say in site selection. 'It was as if the Conquistadores had returned,' remembers the Foundation's technical director.

Eventually, in 1982, the search came to an end with the locating of two adjacent plots of land in the suburban sector of La Enea. The plots measured about 3,000 square metres each, and were well situated. They were off a main road, near the local bus terminal and relatively near a school, a health centre and a children's playground. A supermarket was under construction nearby, as well as a very large government low-cost housing estate. Services were easily accessible, and there were no apparent obstacles to securing the necessary building and services approvals. The fact that Fundemos was dealing with smaller municipal authorities than AVP was to its advantage.

The land identified would allow for the construction of about 94 dwellings. This would do for a start, it was decided. A deposit was paid early in 1982, and the first self-help work began on clearing the site immediately afterwards.

Finance

In keeping with the principles of the project, it was initially expected – in the feasibility study done in 1982 – that at least 30 per cent of the total cost of the scheme would be met from members' own resources, more or less as follows:

	Pesos per member
Initial one-off payments	60,000 (19%)
Monthly payments (initially 200 pesos per month)	2,500 (1%)
Special payments (from employers' bonuses, pensions, etc.)	12,000 (4%)
Self-help labour contribution (90 work-days per family)	30,000 (10%)
Loan funding (15 years repayment)	205,500 (66%)
Total	310,000

As the project got underway, however, it became evident that the initial projected costs were too low to produce the kind of dwelling that members wanted. In consultation with the committee, monthly payments were raised, and further special payments required. Eventually a dwelling costing 400,000 pesos (including finishes and basic furnishing) was arrived at, where nearly 50 per cent of the cost was met by members' financial and self-help contributions, supplemented with the proceeds of fund-raising raffles organised by the Foundation.

Government loan

Loan finance was provided by a pioneering arrangement with the Instituto de Credito Territorial. In late 1982 Fundemos approached ICT to enquire about the possibility of a direct loan to enable it to build with the community. The initial response was that ICT's current regulations did not allow it to make subsidised loans to non-profit organisations. It could, however, make loans to private developers contracted to build low-cost dwellings for persons nominated by ICT – this was the loans to developers scheme. It could also make individual subsidised loans to owner-occupiers to enable them to build or buy their own homes.

Fundemos painstakingly compiled an application to meet the regulations relating to loans to private developers, making available the plethora of documents required for such an application: maps, plans, land surveys and certificates from the service authorities to say these could be provided. Eventually, the application went to the Caldas office of ICT, who recommended its acceptance, pointing out that construction costs by the Fundemos system were 40 per cent lower than equivalent government schemes in the same area, which used private contractors.

The application then had to be forwarded to the central office of ICT in Bogota where it had to be approved in turn by various departments. The technical department approved it after several design and structural alterations – it operated a different set of regulations to the municipal planning office in Manizales. These alterations involved several visits by members of the technical team to Bogota. The application was then passed on to the legal department, which wanted to check all Fundemos' registration documents, deeds for the land, and building and service approvals. Finally, it was lodged with the financial department, for processing when money was available. This went on through most of 1983.

At the end of the year, when a decision seemed imminent, ICT made a 'policy decision' that self-help organisations should not be funded through the loans to developers regulations, but through a kind of pool of the individual loans. Presumably this meant the finance would be drawn from the pool allocated for individual loans and not from that intended for subsidising private developers. It also meant re-presenting the project in a totally different format, more paperwork and more visits to Bogota. The details of each individual member of the project would now have to be vetted, since in theory the funding would be provided by loans to individuals (although in practice a lump sum would be loaned to the Foundation).

The procedure was cumbersome, to say the least, but getting this far had already involved a series of demonstrations, political pressures and string-pulling by the Foundation and its supporters, so there was no turning back. The money for a first phase was eventually paid over in 1984, more than a year after the application was first made. By this time, on the basis of members' contributions and proceeds from the raffle of two houses built with its own resources, Fundemos had funded the installation of the infrastructure and foundations for the entire development.

In spite of the difficulties involved in securing government funding, this pioneering loan was a major breakthrough for Fundemos and the self-help movement. It showed how subsidised government resources and self-help effort could be combined to produce a more appropriate, cost-effective solution, at a lower cost.

Exterior design

Given the size of the plots of land involved, there was little leeway for innovation in the design of the settlement. One of the plots was long and narrow, and in that the architects opted for three parallel terraces of small houses: one facing the main road; the second back-to-back with the first and facing a pedestrian footpath that divided the plot; and the third on the other side of the footpath and facing the second. A playground was situated at one end of this third row. The second plot consisted of two terraces of back-to-backs, separated by a pedestrian footpath, and facing onto main roads on either side.

Several social amenities were also provided: a small community house, where meetings, further education courses, health surgeries and other activities could be held; and frontages for four shops. There was also one playground and some small green areas – totalling 18 per cent of the land used.

Interior design

Because future residents were involved in the scheme from the start, the architects were able to involve them in the design of the dwellings. This consultation was fairly informal, based on discussing drawings and three-dimensional models. The prototype eventually arrived at was that of a more or less conventional, two-storey single family house. Rooms in these houses and houses in the terraces were on the whole tightly packed together to make maximum use of all available space. Maximising space appears to have been the main preoccupation.

Each house had three bedrooms (one on the ground floor and two on the top floor), a living/dining room, a kitchen, a cement-floored patio and an upstairs bathroom. It was designed to allow for future building of one more bedroom (upstairs, over the kitchen) and one more bathroom (in the patio).

Construction technology

Villa Fundemos was built on the basis of conventional building technology, since this was judged to be the most suited to Fundemos' level of experience, capacity for production of building materials, and availability of unskilled and semi-skilled labour.

Foundations were dug by hand and filled with a mixture of stone and cement. The houses were built on these foundations, supported on reinforced concrete columns and beams. Floors were made out of pre-cast concrete slabs, placed after the structure was erected. Infill was provided by cement/sand blocks manufactured at the materials workshop. Floors were either mortar with a vinyl or carpet cover, or wood. The roofing material initially used was Techoline, a French-manufactured asphaltic sheet. Subsequently a fibre-cement roofing sheet, made at the Fundemos workshop, was introduced. Inside and outside doors and door frames – wood and metal respectively – and window frames in metal were also manufactured directly by Fundemos.

Drainage and services networks were put in by the Foundation and its members. The main sewerage outlet was dug by hand as one of the earlier self-help exercises. Wiring and plumbing (to specifications) were installed by Foundation employees with members' help.

Self-building

Although Fundemos employed skilled contractors for certain operations, the majority of work was done by brigades of self-builders. Each family was obliged to give a minimum of 90 days work towards the building of the houses, which was deducted from the cost of each house at the nominal value of a minimum daily wage, per day worked (about 350 pesos – then the equivalent of £1.20).

Members carrying out their work quota were organised into small work teams, or brigades, under the supervision of a semi-skilled co-ordinator, each with a particular job to carry out within an allotted time and to be tackled in whichever way the brigade saw fit. The co-ordinators of the different brigades met together regularly to agree work programmes and sort out difficulties, under the supervision of the site manager. The site manager in turn liaised with the Foundation's architect on work standards and progress.

Brigades could also be allotted work in the workshop, producing prefabricated building parts or manufacturing blocks and roofing sheets.

As in AVP, self-help shifts were intended to promote community spirit and companionship, and were usually energetic, sociable events.

Allocation of finished houses

Allocation was made on the basis of seniority on the project, an agreed level of direct payments and self-help labour having been contributed. Like similar projects elsewhere in Colombia, the individual users become the owners of their dwellings as soon as they move in, beginning to pay off the remaining mortgage to ICT. This repayment can take up to 15 years, during which subsidised interest rates (of about 21 per cent per annum growing by 15 per cent a year) are paid. The initial monthly payment after occupation will be something like 3,500 pesos. For most residents it would mean paying less than they had been paying in rent beforehand.

Once the houses were completed the members' committee continued to function as a neighbourhood council, or JAC, dealing with future needs of the community.

Production of building materials

Shortly after its founding, Fundemos negotiated a long-term lease for a disused railway station in nearby Villamaria. The building was a sturdy old structure on a wooden frame building, with a clay tile roof badly in need of renovation. It was set in 8,000 square metres of sloping land, near a river rich in sand and pebbles. A nearby disused smelter was a potential source of an alternative aggregate, ash. A call to members and sympathisers resulted in the basic repair of the old building, the installation of services and the repair of its only access road. Once a basic decision had been made about the construction technology to be used in the housing scheme, the first machine for manufacture of concrete blocks was installed, and experiments carried out as to appropriate mixes.

As the housing project got underway in 1982, more block-making machines were installed, the new ones manufactured directly by Fundemos with the help of a local metal workshop. All machines used for the manufacture of building materials were low-technology, hand-powered machines (with the exception of power vibrators used for compacting), so they could eventually be built by the group itself.

A variety of prefabricated building parts for the housing project was produced in this workshop, including metal reinforced beams, concrete supports, tiles for roads and paths, floor slabs, structural wall reinforced slabs and concrete sinktops. Fundemos has also researched and developed its own synthetic plaster, made from a mixture of glue, talc and colorants, which was used in the housing project to give a smooth finish over cement blocks.

The workshop was run by a small technical team employed by Fundemos, which experimented with and developed the various processes. The workshop made use of self-help labour, however, for the production of large quantities of blocks or prefabricated elements for the housing project.

As a result of a training scheme carried out in 1983 by Intermediate Technology Workshops (J. P. M. Parry & Associates Ltd), Fundemos developed a method for the production of roofing sheets on an 'in situ' basis. The process involved a mixture of cement, sand, ash and natural or plastic fibre, vibrated on a metal table for consistency, and then moulded over a corrugated template. Houses built later were roofed with this material.

An interesting sideline of this work is that the workshop has branched out into the production of 'low-tech' machines for the production of building materials. At the moment it is able to manufacture block-making machines, roofing sheet machines and a number of moulds for reinforced beams, slabs and other building components.

The workshop at Villamaria has become a kind of 'appropriate technology' centre for organisations affiliated to Fedevivienda. In December 1984 the first national workshop on Appropriate Building Technology was held there, with delegates from several associations throughout the country. As a result the idea of setting up a School of Self-Help Housing was launched, based around the Manizales workshop, where technical staff and organisers of self-help schemes all over the country could be trained in practical aspects of building materials production and self-build house construction, as well as other aspects of organising such projects.

Community projects

Health. This was the first project in Fundemos to become operative. It began simply as a medical surgery and small pharmacy operating from the Fundemos office. People on low incomes could sign up for a nominal fee, and receive treatment which would be paid for at a nominal rate. Dental treatment was later added to this facility.

In 1982 the project was expanded to include a laboratory and some basic training courses in first aid and health promotion for volunteers. The subscription fee was raised, and fuller medical services were provided. Thus the scheme became a kind of health insurance for members. Early in 1983, a donation from a German charity 'Bread for the World', allowed this medical programme to expand. At that time it had 500 subscription-paying members.

The next year 'health brigades' were formed, made up of professionals and trained volunteers, to visit poorer districts and deal with pressing health requirements. These tours have been repeated twice a month since then, and now include housing and education advisors who try to help residents with problems in all these spheres.

Education. Fundemos' educational programme has been primarily geared to adult education, with an emphasis on women's training. There has also been 'vocational' training within the various projects being carried out – building (with help from SENA – the government training institute), health promotion, nutrition and first aid. Some courses have been geared to teaching useful skills with possible income value such as accountancy, dressmaking, hairdressing or cooking. Others have merely attempted to raise the general cultural level of the community like those in art, music, social sciences and politics. Much emphasis has also been placed on the training of community organisers in the principles of self-management and self-reliance. In 1986 Fundemos estimated that over 1,000 people had so far received training from the Foundation.

One interesting extra-mural project undertaken by this project has been the organising of a self-build input for a local primary school which was lacking funds for a much needed extension of its facilities. Ten additional classrooms have been built by parents and volunteers.

Ecology. In 1982 Fundemos founded its ecology project. Its first activity was to arrange an exhibition of natural resources and dangers facing them, with the Fundacion Ecologica Autonoma, a local pressure group. It has subsequently co-operated with Inderena, the government natural resources protection agency, the local authority and a number of ecological youth clubs on local campaigns. In 1984 it participated in the creation of an 'Ecological Centre' to monitor erosion in the area, with Inderena and a local 'Campaign Against Erosion'.

Other activities

Fundemos has been very effective in publicising its activities and gaining support for its work. It has succeeded in getting sympathetic press and radio coverage of its activities and has also had very good contact with local politicians, and fielded a candidate at the recent parliamentary elections.

The Foundation has been a major influence, in spite of its relatively small size, in the development of Fedevivienda, and is especially recognised for its work in the field of appropriate technology for self-help. This contribution has become more central since the setting up, in 1985, of the National School for Self-Help Housing based on the Manizales building workshop. The school has so far run a number of short residential courses for Fedevivienda members and people wanting to initiate new projects, and has recently received a donation of £33,000 from International Year of Shelter for the Homeless (UK) for equipment.

Fundemos has also been very successful in the field of independent fund-raising, bringing in extra capital by organising raffles, banquets and other events, and even more from donations from public, private and international agencies. It has demonstrated that many additional resources can be available to organisations that are willing and able to look for them.

Since 1985, when the first phase of Villafundemos was complete, the Foundation has initiated another project in the nearby district of Riosucio. This has served to consolidate Fundemos' 'secondary' role. And after the horrifying disaster of the Ruiz Volcano, when 22,000 people were killed by its sudden eruption, Fundemos participated in the relief operations for the victims of this tragedy in the area. As an offshoot of this a further self-build project – Llanitos – was carried out with families who had lost their homes in the disaster.

Summary

Fundemos is an example of a successful, independent self-help housing project, initiated by a group of committed professionals who helped bring a community together to build their own homes. It was developed on a relatively small scale, in the belief that this would be the best start for an organisation with no previous housing experience. It was funded directly by members and by subsidised government loans, and made use of intermediate technologies and self-build for construction.

About half the cost of the project was met from savings and special payments by members, and extra funds were also raised by the Foundation. The rest was financed by subsidised 15-year loans given by ICT to individual members. Having access to subsidy, as well as other ways of raising cash, meant that the project could provide good-quality housing for people on very low incomes. The cost of a Fundemos house represented a saving of more than 40 per cent on the cost of a government-built equivalent.

Land had to be found on the open market, and this was done in consultation with future residents who also visited potential sites. Because of the small size of the project it was only possible to purchase enough land for about 100 dwellings, and no land stock for future development was built up. Future projects will inevitably find land more expensive and harder to get.

Internal drains and service networks were installed directly by the Foundation, using self-build brigades and contract labour. Work on these went ahead without delays, in contrast to projects where municipal authorities have been responsible for their provision. Also, local authorities work on a smaller scale, and are probably more accessible, in a medium-size city like Manizales than they would be in larger cities.

Having come from a background of aiding informal settlements, the organisers of Fundemos learnt from their earlier mistakes. Unnecessary clashes with the authorities (over by-laws or regulations) have been avoided by sound professional back-up, and the use of legal channels pioneered. Members' energy has not been wasted in futile demonstrations and confrontations (although a fair amount has been consumed by red tape) and their real contributions have been co-ordinated to the best effect.

The legal framework used by Fundemos to develop the project, like that of similar projects, was not ideal, but just about adequate. No serious complications were encountered in developing the project, apart from the considerable red tape involved in obtaining ICT funding. This went as far as requiring alterations to plans that had already been approved by the local planning office, as well as the collection of much irrelevant information.

Fundemos initially (correctly) defined this type of activity as a collaboration between two distinct but mutually dependent groups: the community that needs housing, and the professionals who can enable them to obtain it. They did not go as far, however, as to suggest the setting-up, from the start, of a distinct community organisation, as a counterpart to the professional one. Instead, they attempted to integrate the 'users' into the structure of the Foundation through an informal members' committee which had no real executive powers. This informal arrangement might have prevented potential power struggles (such as AVP experienced), but it did not create a concrete basis for the Foundation's accountability to users. As a result participation was often vague and superficial, and amounted to little more than opinions and comments on potential sites, layouts, house designs and methods of organising self-build. This shortcoming was partly the product of the way the community was brought together (on the initiative of the development body), but also of the fact that no precedent existed in the country for communities participating directly in design and development of their housing. The role of the members' committee was, therefore, limited to encouraging users to contribute to the project, in terms of money and labour, and to ensuring that self-build took place within the agreed regulations, only marginally providing a channel for feedback from members.

With hindsight, the creation of an independent community structure from the start, combined with a more formal arrangement between community organisation and development body (in the form of a development agreement), as well as the application of more effective methods of informing and involving members in design and development, might have led to a more effective collaboration.

Apart from this, methods of self-building were practical and effective. Technologies were found and developed which allowed for considerable self-reliance in building, and created future employment opportunities. These were not 'vernacular' technologies (which would probably require more skills), but conventional ones at an appropriate scale, using simple machines and accessible materials, and adequate for unskilled self-builders. The organisation of self-build on the basis of small, semi-independent brigades was also effective, allowing for group initiative within a structured programme.

Overall control and administration of the project was in the hands of the Fundemos technical team, reducing the bureaucracy to a minimum. The government's role was limited to providing a (barely adequate) legal framework within which the group could operate, planning and building controls, and providing services and loan funding needed to complete the project. Of these, the requirements involved in securing funding turned out to be the greatest problem, delaying the project by about a year. This was partly due to ICT's lack of coherent strategy for dealing with these groups.

The dwellings have been allocated to those members who are up to date in payments and work quotas, and individual houses have been chosen by lot. Each property is fully owned by its occupier, having been paid for by a combination of work, direct payments, and a 15-year loan. An alternative 'community leasehold' arrangement considered at one stage (where the Foundation would own a share of the property and sell it to individual occupiers on the basis of small monthly payments over a 15-year period was ruled out by ICT's policy of not giving loans to organisations. This option might have helped ensure better management and maintenance, and prevented speculative sales. Rental was never considered a possibility in view of the high initial contribution made by residents.

One important factor in the Fundemos housing project being able to get this far has been the political influence it has developed, mainly as a result of its work on community services and issues. It has succeeded in obtaining some support from local politicians and traditional parties (particularly the local Liberal Party), but has so far avoided being manipulated by these groups and becoming another 'client' organisation. It remains independent and therein lies a good part of the reason for its success.

12 | Conclusions

My main intention in undertaking the research that led up to this book was to record thoughts and observations from over 14 years' involvement with community housing, and to try to make some sense out of them. At the same time, I have tried to draw on written accounts of similar projects, so that other experiences could be brought in to complement my own, and conclusions drawn from both.

So as to not look at projects in a vacuum, I have attempted, within the limitations of time and resources, to look at the background factors that helped to shape all the events described. I would not claim that these accounts are exhaustive, or that they are not partisan. Although I have tried to state both the positive and the negative aspects of each project described, it is not difficult to see where my sympathies lie. I fully admit to being biased in favour of community housing.

This final chapter attempts to look at these experiences in a more abstract context. I will attempt to draw out some general observations regarding community participation in housing, its methods, its strengths and pitfalls, and its possibilities for the future. If individual case histories are examples of 'principles in action', it is useful to try to identify those principles, and the methods that incorporate them, so that other projects can be viewed in this light and future projects be guided by them.

Historical factors

Pre-industrial, informal and capital-based housing. In both Britain and Colombia pre-industrial (or pre-capitalist) housing practices were primarily 'participatory'. Families built with their own labour and resources, using local materials and traditional techniques. For skilled tasks, artisans might be employed, and more difficult jobs might involve co-operation within the community. But each family was very much in control of its own resources and how they were used. The limitations of the housing produced was set by the resources available and the skills of the builders, rather than by external regulation. This situation, which was the norm in rural areas in both countries, changed dramatically as a result of industrialisation and the growth of urban centres.

In Britain this took place during the Industrial Revolution. Migrant families arriving in urban centres rarely had the capital to buy land and building materials, so self-building was out of the question. Production of low-income housing was taken over by private landlords, who provided densely-packed housing for rent. Returns on this investment were possible thanks to the wages paid to the new labouring class. But users lost the measure of control over their housing that they had in the pre-industrial period.

In Colombia, with an economy traditionally dependent on the export of raw materials and the import of manufactured goods, industrialisation did not really begin until the Great Depression limited exports to the industrialised nations. Investment was then redirected into local consumer industries, mainly for the limited internal market. Markets were limited so investment was limited. Much capital was foreign, so what profits were made did not remain in the country. Little employment was created and wages were generally low.

A consequence of this was that private investment was not available to take over the task of providing low-income housing. Urban labourers, usually employed in craft trades or services, could not pay the level of rents necessary to make such investment worthwhile. The result was that they were obliged to continue relying on pre-industrial self-help housing practices to put a roof over their heads. This sometimes involved squatting or purchasing cheap, 'illegal' land on the black market and building for themselves and, increasingly, for others. Over the years this 'informal' sector has grown and provided the majority of the country's low-income housing. It has adopted commercial techniques and materials in preference to traditional ones, and commercial relationships in preference to traditional communal practices.

Similarly, in Britain, when economic slumps have depressed incomes and public housing provision has been cut back, whole sections of society have been obliged to revert to informal housing practices, such as squatting and self-building.

Urban conflicts and state provision. As urban centres grew at an accelerated rate (in Britain in the 1800s, in Colombia in the mid-1900s), a struggle ensued between the rich and the poor for access to, and control of, housing resources. This is most clearly reflected in persistent conflicts over the different parts of the city.

In Britain, low-income groups gravitated towards the central and industrial areas of Victorian cities, in an effort to be 'near their bread'. In doing so, they often displaced wealthier sections of society, who moved to healthier, suburban areas. But when land used for working-class housing was required for a financially important redevelopment, such as for roads or railways, or when conditions in these areas became a general health risk, the State would intervene, with closure and clearance powers. Such intervention was widespread in Britain at the turn of the century, and was usually not resisted, perhaps because it was often directed against unpopular private landlords. As a result of this intervention municipal authorities were obliged to provide housing directly for the victims of slum clearance.

In Colombia, a similar conflict arose in the 1930s. State intervention was not directed against small landlords, but against large, informal settlements. This made intervention difficult and often violent since from all accounts people were prepared to defend their own homes. Apart from this, the State lacked resources to provide alternative housing. Intervention was thus kept to a minimum and the informal sector was allowed to grow, as long as it did not overrun the wealthier areas. The results are evident in most Third World cities today.

Early State intervention determined the nature of State provision in both countries. In Britain, thanks to the parliamentary nature of national and local government, and the strength of organised workers, the Labour Party seized control of the apparatus of municipal housing and used it to provide large numbers of subsidised dwellings, to usually high standards and primarily for the employed working class. But the paternalistic approach characteristic of early municipal intervention became a permanent feature of council housing.

In Colombia, State intervention in informal settlements was small, and provision equally insignificant. Only at times of potential political upheaval (such as in the years following the Cuban revolution) was there any real attempt to expand public sector provision, using US aid and 'aided' self-help. But these loans proved inflationary, and self-help practices unpopular with the powerful vested interests. They were soon dropped in favour of extending subsidies to private builders to build a small number of houses for sale to families on middle incomes.

Britain too has been obliged to reduce public housing expenditure, partly as a result of the inflationary burden of international loans undertaken in the past, which today accounts for much of the rental income from council housing stock.

The decline of provision and the search for alternatives. There have been other reasons, apart from financial constraints, for the loss of support for direct State provision experienced in both countries. One is the failure of this method to provide the type of housing that people want and need. Although this is sometimes explained as a result of not using 'enough' technology, or not spending 'enough', the problem goes deeper than that. Because of the way they have developed, State housing authorities in both countries have become distant public firms, which promote housing programmes based on ideological, financial and/or technical considerations, rather than the real needs and aspirations of future users.

In Britain, the parliamentary nature of local government ensures that public housing is indirectly accountable to its users. But this is usually limited to voting for abstract policies, targets and standards, and does not involve any real consultation to determine preferences. In practice decisions are left to professionals, under the financial eye of civil servants and the guidance of politicians.

In Colombia, even such limited accountability is out of the question, and housing authorities have been relegated to the role of State building societies, using subsidised loan funds to finance the building (by private developers) of mass housing projects, or simply to subsidise owner-occupation.

It is understandable, therefore, that community-based housing initiatives became increasingly popular in both countries. These initiatives are nothing new: In Victorian England 'blood for blood' self-build ventures provided housing for some tradesmen and their families. In Colombia, the housing co-operatives of the 1930s, some of which still survive, provided housing for the middle class.

Because they operated within a commercial framework and without access to public resources, these initiatives were unable to reach the people with the greatest housing need. Also, they were usually regarded with hostility by the early supporters of direct provision.

Recently, this opposition has turned to support. The Colombian government, in the late 1950s, supported the setting up of neighbourhood organisations which later provided the basis for the development of the present self-help housing movement. This movement was further boosted in the 1980s by new laws and additional public and private investment. But to date, in spite of nominal government support, self-help housing organisations still have to battle for survival.

In Britain, the State has always given some support to the 'voluntary' sector, although this support has been primarily directed towards the large paternalist trusts rather than the small, democratic co-operatives. In the 1960s this support was channelled through the Housing Corporation, and taken a step further in 1974 with the introduction of the HAG system of funding. Both the supervisory role of the Corporation, however, and the characteristics of the funding system have encouraged a tendency towards monopoly in favour of large housing associations, while the future of community-based housing associations and co-ops remains uncertain.

It is likely, therefore, that community housing initiatives and community control of housing will continue to develop in both countries. But it is also possible, in both countries, that this development will be sidetracked, for political reasons, into a drive to increase owner-occupation. It is also possible that State support for the voluntary sector will be directed primarily towards large, paternalist housing organisations to the exclusion of the community-based initiatives, bringing us back, full-circle, to an even less accountable form of provision from the top down. The outcome will largely depend on the clarity, cohesion and determination of the movement in both countries in years to come.

Principles

From a study of the case histories and their backgrounds, it appears that several basic principles consistently recur, and these are worth highlighting before going into further detail. These are the following:

The need to form communities. We all once lived in natural communities. These communities were essential for our survival, ensuring access to food, companionship and survival. Capitalism and the growth of the cities destroyed these communities, isolating individuals, throwing them into competition for jobs, or for housing, in the interests of financial gain. Growth of representative democracy in Britain allowed the Labour Party to determine use of public resources for housing, but did not give workers direct control of those resources. This control can only be created by a third stage of development, where communities of users are vested with collective management of those resources, within an overall plan. For this to happen, the development of genuine, self-managing communities is a basic pre-condition.

The need for a nurturing framework. For a community housing organisation to form and develop, it needs access to resources and professional skills, and to the forms of organisation that will allow it continued control of its environment. Sometimes organisations can make use of an unofficial (or illegal) framework to develop, but such frameworks are rarely ideal. Official frameworks which are geared towards giving support to community self-organisation can be valuable, as long as they are not used primarily as a way of manipulating the movement, or as long as the movement is strong enough to resist such manipulation. The ideal of a completely 'enabling' framework, with no strings, is probably utopian . . .

Community control of resources. When control of resources is vested in the community, rather than in each individual or on State organisations, a more balanced and appropriate use of those resources is likely to result. Obviously, such control is only possible when a community is sufficiently organised and the framework sufficiently supportive for self-management to occur. Even having the possibility of control, a community will not be able to exercise it without 'enabling' professional support. This level of direct control will probably be impossible to maintain without structural safeguards and regular checks to ensure that control has not been appropriated by the organisers or the professionals helping the scheme.

Professional services should be 'enabling'. That is, they should help users to learn and to make decisions, rather than mystifying and excluding them, and making the decisions for them. Working with a community does not mean just studying it. It implies securing its participation in the various administrative, financial and technical decisions needed throughout the process. For people to be thus involved, they have to be trained in all basic aspects of the housing process. This is a fundamental departure from the paternalist methods of traditional housing provision, and is not likely to come easily to housing professionals. It is probably more viable through the creation of professional secondary housing organisations, which in turn are accountable to the primary community organisations.

Designs, technologies and forms of organisation should be selected by the community, to ensure they meet real needs and possibilities. This naturally follows from the above. If the framework promotes the training of the users and encourages them to make the decisions required in shaping their environment, then it is likely that the choices made will be the most appropriate within the potential and aspirations of that community. Through these 'tailor-made' choices, the wasteful and socially destructive mistakes of the past will, it is to be hoped, be avoided.

The aim of professional enabling and a supportive framework is to maximise choice. A community can only decide what is the best use of resources to meet its needs if it is given as wide as possible a range of choices, at every level and at every stage of the process. Equally, they must be made aware of the implications of each choice. This is the total opposite of traditional housing provision, where all the choices are made for the user by somebody else.

These general principles contain most of the lessons from the successful projects studied. We will now look in detail at what those principles mean in practice.

Participants, resources and the process

Participants. There are three main participants in any housing project. They are the **community**, the **professionals** and the **resource bodies**.

Within any particular project, the **community** can be at different stages of development, and demonstrate different degrees of organisation and internal cohesion. Very few communities of users are entirely self-organised, most are brought together by local authorities or by secondary housing organisations. The degree of control exercised by users, and whether that control increases or declines with time, also differs from one experience to another. But in every case the existence of a clearly-defined community organisation, with a separate identity distinct from professional and government bodies, was a precondition of real control.

The **professionals** are also an essential ingredient, since they provide the necessary administrative, financial and technical support to the communities concerned. But professionals hold a monopoly of expertise which gives them a powerful position in these projects, and will often tend to take control of projects 'on behalf of' the users. Only when professionals are persuaded of the importance of user-control, and of the community itself as the client – rather than the State or the secondary – is their intervention likely to be enabling.

The **resource bodies** are the 'external' participants in the project, determining the framework and providing the necessary resources for the project. The framework determines the form that the community and the project take, and the support or obstacles that will be given or put in its way. Resources, such as land and finance, are usually made available with a series of regulations, cost-limits and building standards, restricting their use. Resource bodies can be public or private, and operate coherently or through a morass of contradictory rules and regulations.

The most enabling intervention a resource body can make is the provision of the necessary resources to the community within flexible limits which are sufficiently broad to give them a range of options in their use. The most disabling one is to limit actions and choices open to community groups, without providing them with any additional resources.

Resources. The resources necessary for carrying out a project can be 'internal', if they are provided by the community itself, or 'external' if they are provided by other bodies. The main resources are **land, infrastructure and services, finance** and **human resources**.

Land is usually an external resource. Most projects in Britain acquired land, and sometimes housing, from the local authority, which subsidised their cost, making access easier. Where such official support was not available, land had to be purchased on the open market. Having to do this raised the cost to the community, but possibly broadened its choice. Organisations in Colombia used the pooled savings of members to purchase land commercially, and even built up their own land banks on this basis.

Infrastructure and services – roads, drainage, electricity and water – are usually external resources, provided by public boards. The provision of these services must be co-ordinated with the construction of the project, and carried out in a quick and efficient manner, if they are not to become an obstacle to the project. Since municipal authorities are usually responsible for this provision, a supportive framework can ensure good liaison between these bodies and the community organisations. Where such co-operation is unlikely, some projects have been prepared to provide these services themselves.

In an age of capital-based housing development, **finance** is a key resource, almost inevitably external. Although some projects, particularly in Colombia, have managed to generate enough finance internally to fund their projects during the initial stages, all projects studied needed loan funding and/or subsidy at some stage. The important factor here is not whether finance is internal or external, subsidised or not, but that control of capital resources rests ultimately with the community, so that it can determine how it is used.

Human resources, both in terms of labour and professional skills, are essential to any housing development. Some communities supplied their own labour without needing to purchase it (self-help labour), and even some professional skills. But most had to purchase these skills. In some cases, professional services were given, as a sort of subsidy, by government bodies. In the most successful instances these were provided by secondary housing organisations set up for this purpose. Again, the key factor is not whether they were external or internal, but how accountable these professional services were to the community of users.

Process. The participants and the resources come together in the housing process, which produces housing. I would divide the main stages of this process into **proposal, organisation** and **development**.

Proposal is the stage when the project, its user group, its size and scope, is determined. The proposal is usually determined by the group that initiates the project. Thus projects initiated by a community usually reflect its real needs and preferences, whereas those initiated by professionals or government bodies are more likely to reflect the interests of those groups.

It may be observed that projects proposed by communities themselves are usually locally based and pitched at a smaller, manageable scale. Projects proposed by professionals and government bodies are larger and often unmanageable. The smaller scale of genuine community projects does not detract from their social value since it is probably more realistic in the long term to develop a variety of small, genuinely accountable local projects, than a few large, unmanageable ones. Economies of scale are not necessarily conducive to successful self-management.

Control of a project at the level of proposal will usually determine its **organisation**. If a community has proposed a project, it will avail itself of accountable professional services to implement it. The existence of specialised secondary organisations will be decisive in this instance.

If, on the other hand, the project is proposed by professionals or government bodies, they will then have to identify, or 'create' a community to use and manage it. Ready-made communities may be found in existing groups, like residents of a clearance area, or formed from the waiting lists of government bodies. If the social engineering involved in forming a community is to be successful, the promoters must ensure that the people brought together have more in common than just needing a place to live. This must involve 'integration activities' where people have a chance to meet, work with and get to know each other prior to occupation. One of the strengths of self-building is that it provides this opportunity.

Ideally, users should eventually develop a separate, autonomous, democratic organisation, which enables them to decide the shape of their housing and to manage it after completion. If the organisation is unstable or divided, control will be erratic or non-existent, and will probably be assumed by the professionals, who are supposed only to be helping the project.

Development of a project takes place from the acquisition of land or housing until the occupation of the housing produced. This stage has two main phases, design and construction.

Effective implementation of development almost inevitably requires the intervention of professionals – at one level, development managers to ensure that the resources are secured and available to allow the project to proceed; at another, consultants to ensure that architectural and technical requirements and standards are met, and to supervise and carry out construction.

Only rarely have communities been able to carry out their own development, and when they have it is usually at a fairly basic level. In some cases development has been managed by the local authority on the community's behalf. More often, development has been carried out by a specialised secondary organisation, which in turn employs consultants and contractors to build. In the best instances, these organisations are accountable to the communities they serve. If a community is to really manage development through its secondary organisation, it must be trained to understand the processes involved and to make the decisions required. Therefore the role of the secondary housing body must be to educate the primary community in all aspects of the housing process.

The first phase of development is design. If the community is non-existent, or in the back seat of the project, the design will be carried out by the architects appointed by the local authority or secondary organisation. If the community is in control, then one of the first functions of the secondary housing organisation will be to help the community select an architect. The architect will then help the community develop designs, decide on building materials and, in self-build, on the technologies to be used and how the work will be organised.

This might involve methods of participation in design such as 3-D models, overhead projection and visits to different types of houses. Samples of different materials can also be looked at. If the works are to be contracted, the architect can help the community choose an appropriate builder. If self-build is involved, the community will have to become familiar with the building technology used. In either case, the architect will usually manage the construction on behalf of the community. If works are contracted this will involve providing specifications and drawings for the works required, and supervising builders in carrying them out. In self-build the architect will usually advise the community on how to organise construction, as well as supervise the actual carrying out of the works.

This might involve organising work brigades to carry out different construction tasks within an overall programme, or supervising the individual families as they build their own houses. If the project is large enough, a site supervisor, or clerk of works, might be employed to supervise the building. As a general principle, using industrial building technologies will require using skilled contractors or organising users into specialised work brigades. Only simpler building technologies, like the Segal timber frame system, will be appropriate for families building on their own.

Whereas using self-help labour can reduce costs and allow families working with limited funds to afford a higher standard of dwelling, the projects employing skilled contractors have a wider choice as far as design, building technologies and materials used. As long as they have the funding to afford it, these groups can concentrate on the results rather than worrying about whether they have the skills to handle a particular building method. Of course, this is only possible where users have high incomes or access to relatively high levels of subsidy.

Some organisations employed direct labour to carry out works, and others relied on parallel building co-operatives or non-profit building teams funded by the Manpower Services Commission to carry out works. The builders might in some cases also be future users. But in every case builders, through the architect, were accountable to the user-group.

Post-development

Participation in development is the first step in a community's management of its own housing. Managing it after development is of course the definitive measure of control. The community organisation will have to deal with allocation of the dwellings, as well as their ongoing management and maintenance. It may delegate or contract these responsibilities to other bodies, but it will often choose to carry them out directly.

Where established community groups proposed the project, they knew from the start who would be housed, and individual dwellings were usually decided at design stage. In other cases, individual allocation of houses was not known until after construction, and decided by lot. In some cases the project was promoted by a secondary organisation, and the users identified after construction was finished. On the whole, the projects which allocated prior to construction seemed to have had the best results.

Re-allocation of vacant dwellings was another matter. Only in those projects where ownership or tenure was collective was re-allocation in the hands of the community. In schemes that were owner-occupied or under co-ownership the re-allocation of the finished dwellings was in the hands of the individual owners, although they would probably require the consent of the co-owner to sell the property. In some cases the local authority, as a condition of support, had maintained nomination rights for up to half the dwellings becoming vacant on the scheme.

As far as the allocation policies applied by each particular group, there is no reason to believe that they would be more (or less) discriminatory than those of any official housing body. More likely, different community housing groups will have a variety of criteria, corresponding to a variety of needs, which will provide for many more individual requirements than centralised allocation priorities could.

Responsibility for management and maintenance functions, and how they were organised and paid for, depended on the particular tenure involved in the scheme. Thus in projects where properties were owner-occupied, owners were responsible for management and maintenance of their own dwellings, although there might be a few collective responsibilities (such as communal areas). In co-ownership arrangements, responsibility for this function was maintained by the co-owning body (the local authority or housing association) and funded from the rental element paid to this body.

If, however, the properties were owned or held collectively by the community, the co-ops or associations were primarily responsible for management and maintenance, and this function financed by the rent paid by each user to this body. Alternatively, the community organisation might choose to employ a 'management agent' (possibly a secondary housing organisation) to carry out this function.

Tenure and costs

The choice of tenure was usually implicit in the type of resources used. If a project was built with the labour of individual members and/or with their savings, it was only natural that they would own at least a part of the housing produced. Some of the projects were therefore owner-occupied or co-owned with the local authority. These projects might also offer the users the possibility of buying the remaining equity in their dwellings.

If, on the other hand, subsidised public funds were used, and labour contracted, the properties would remain the property of the community organisation, with individual residents being both landlords and tenants. This at least ensured that the property remained in public ownership, and accessible to other low-income people.

One project did not own properties at all, but merely managed properties owned by other bodies.

The cost of housing in all the projects studied was kept low by the non-profit nature of the organisations concerned. In some projects the costs to the community were further reduced by the use of self-help labour, and by access to subsidy. A number of projects, both in Britain and Colombia, showed reductions of over 40 – 50 per cent on comparable commercial costs. Those which did not attempt to reduce costs showed increased standards of design and construction.

Subsidy and self-help are therefore not mutually exclusive, but complementary. Both can lower costs or improve quality. One possible advantage of having both in participatory housing projects is that the community can then choose whether it wants higher standards or lower costs, or a balance between the two.

The benefits

Apart from the obvious contribution to the provision of social housing, there are various benefits to all participants arising from these projects.

Individual users are helped to integrate into communities which can become effective instruments in meeting other social needs. This is particularly evident where complementary community projects, involving non-housing activities, have been promoted. Having a say in the design and building of their own homes invariably gives people confidence and encourages them to have a greater say in society and their environment.

Professionals benefit from having the opportunity to develop new skills in a challenging way of producing good social housing. As a result of these initiatives, new techniques have been developed for involving users in design, for self-building, for training and informing future users, and these have become new tools for the professional. A new approach based on enabling is now recognised as, for instance, what is described as community architecture.

Resource bodies and government also benefit from the new models of public housing developed from these experiences. These new models are a definite advance on the rigid traditional models, and are more likely to produce the type of housing that people want and need, and to avoid the costly mistakes of direct provision.

In conclusion, although the present trend towards participation might be reminiscent of the pre-industrial housing practices of the past, the projects I have described demonstrate the practices of the future, combining advanced technology and resources with direct control by users themselves. In both Britain and Colombia, participation in housing is a dynamic expression of the drive by ordinary people to regain control of those resources necessary for survival and happiness, a control which was lost in the advance of modern industrial society. Rather than expressing a wish to escape into the past, they represent a decisive step into the future.

Bibliography

Arango, Carlos. *La Lucha por la Vivienda en Colombia* (1986). Edicions Eco, Bogota.

Anderson, Hugh. 'Appraisal' in *Architects' Journal* 18 July 1984.

Arscott, Mary-Lou et al. *Alternatives in Housing? A Report on Self-Build in Britain* (1976). Architectural Association, London.

Bailey, Ron. *The Squatters* (1977). Penguin, London.

Bailey, Ron. *The Homeless and the Empty Houses* (1977). Penguin, London.

Bailey, Ron, and Ruddock, Joan. *The Grief Report* (1972). Shelter, London.

Bartholomew, Ron. 'West London Secondary' in *Around the Houses* 1986 No 13. NFHC, London.

Benwell C.D.P. *Private Housing and the Working Class* (1978). Russell Press, Nottingham.

Berry, Fred. *Housing, the Great British Failure* (1974). Charles Knight, London.

Bloor, Tony. 'Glasgow: Community Ownership Co-operatives' (1985). *Around the Houses* No 11, August. NFHC, London.

Bluestein, Howard et al. *Area Handbook for Colombia* (1977). The American University, Washington DC.

Boddy, Martin. *The Building Societies* (1980). Macmillan, London.

Campbell, Harold. *Housing Co-ops – After Ten Years* (1985). The Co-operative Party, London.

Campaign for Homes in Central London. *City Life: A Future for Central London* (1986). London.

Caradog Jones, D.(ed) *The Social Survey of Merseyside* (1934). University Press of Liverpool, Hodder and Stoughton, London.

Castells, Manuel. *The Urban Question* (1977). Edward Arnold, London.

Chambers, Charlotte et al. *Comparative Study of Secondary Housing Co-operatives* (1985). Polytechnic of Central London, London.

Christiansen, Susanne P. *Housing and Improvement – A Comparative Study Britain-Denmark* (1983). Unpublished dissertation, Institute of Advanced Architectural Studies, University of York.

Clay, Jonathan et al. *Tenants Rule – Lessons for Greenwich from Glasgow's Tenant Management Housing Co-operatives* (1986). Consultative Document, Housing Department, London Borough of Greenwich, London.

Coleman, Alice. *Utopia on Trial: Vision and Reality in Planned Housing* (1985). Hilary Shipman, London.

Conway, Joan and Kemp, Peter. *Bed and Breakfast: Slum Housing of the Eighties* (1985). SHAC, London.

Co-operative Development Services. *Annual Report 1984-85* (1985). London.

Co-operative Development Services. *Building Democracy* (1985). Liverpool.

Cowley, John. *Housing for People or Profit* (1979) Stage 1, London.

Darke, Jane and Roy. *Who Needs Council Housing?* (1979). Macmillan, London.

Davies, Chris. 'Liverpool Co-ops – The Liberal View' in *Voluntary Housing* Vol 16 No 3. NFHA, London.

Devas, Nick. *Indonesia's Kampung Improvement Programme: An Evaluative Case Study* (1980). Development Administration Group, Institute of Local Government Studies, University of Birmingham.

Ellis, Charlotte. 'Do-It-Yourself Vernacular' in *Architects' Journal* (17 December 1980).

Edwards, Michael. 'Cities of Tenants: Renting among the Urban Poor in Latin America' in *Urbanisation in Contemporary Latin America* A.Gilbert, J.E. Hardy, R.Ramirez (eds) (1982). John Wiley, Chichester.

Fedevivienda. *Memorias del Primer Congreso* (1983). Fedevivienda, Bogota.

Gilbert, Alan, and Gugler, Joseph. *Cities, Poverty and Development – Urbanisation in the Third World* (1982). Oxford University Press, Oxford.

Gilbert, Alan, and Ward, Peter. 'Low Income Housing and the

State' in *Urbanisation in Contemporary Latin America* (see above).
Greater London Council. *Community Areas Policy – A Record of Development* (1985). GLC, London.
Greeve, John. *Homelessness in London* (1971). Centre for Urban and Regional Studies, University of Birmingham.
Greeve, John. *London's Homeless* (1964). Codicote Press, Welwyn.
Grieve, Sir Robert et al. *Inquiry into Housing in Glasgow* (1985). Glasgow District Council, Glasgow.
Grosskurth, Anne. 'Bringing Back the Braddocks' in *Roof* January 1985. Shelter.
Hands, John. *Housing Co-operatives* (1975). Society for Co-operative Dwellings, London.
Harrison, Paul. *The Third World Tomorrow* (1980). Penguin, London.
Holt, Pat. *Colombia Today and Tomorrow* (1964). Pall Mall Press, London.
Horowitz, Irving. 'Electoral Politics, Urbanisation and Social Development in Latin America' in *Latin American Radicalism: A Documentary Report on Left and Nationalistic Movements* I. Horowitz, J. de Castro and J. Gerassi (eds) (1969). Vintage, New York.
Housing Associations Consultancy and Advisory Service. *Interim Report on the Society for Co-operative Dwellings* (1985). London.
Housing Corporation. *Improving Your Performance: A Report on the Result of Monitoring Visits by the Housing Corporation* (1986).
Housing Corporation. *Services to Housing Co-operatives in South and West London* (1985).
Illich, Ivan. 'Disabling Professions' in *Disabling Professions* (1978). 'Ideas in Progress' series, Open Forum, Marion Boyars, London.
Ingham, Andrew. *Self-Help House Repair Manual* (1977). Penguin, London.
Innes Wilkin, David. 'Architect's Account' in *Architects' Journal* 18 July 1984.
International Labour Office. *Housing Co-operatives* (1964). Geneva.
Janssen, Roel. *Vivienda y Luchas Populares en Bogota* (1984). Editorial Tercer Mundo, Bogota.
Jaramillo, Samuel. *Produccion de Vivienda y Capitalismo Dependiente – el Caso de Bogota* (1979). CEDE, Facultad de Economia, Universidad de los Andes, Bogota.

Johnson, Jim. 'Public Management of the Private Sector' in *Architects' Journal* 20 August 1986.

Krajwska, Sophy. 'How It All Began' in *Architects' Journal* 18 July 1984.

Langstaff, Michael. 'The Changing Role of Housing Associations' in *The Planner* 1984.

Lansley, Stuart. 'The Growing Housing Crisis' in *The Right to a Home* (1984). Labour Housing Group, Spokesman Press, Nottingham.

Leopold, Margaret. 'Red Skirts on the Clydeside' in *Housetalk* Spring 1984. The Housetalk Group, Glasgow.

McDonald, Alan. *The Weller Way* (1986). Faber and Faber, London.

McGurn, Logan and Duncan. *Calvay Housing Co-operative – Feasibility Study* (1984). Glasgow District Council, Glasgow.

McKnight, John. 'Professionalised Service and Disabling Help' in *Disabling Professions* (1978). Marion Boyars, London.

McLennan, Duncan et al. *The Activities and Effectiveness of Housing Associations in Scotland 1974-1980* (1981). Preliminary Report, Scottish Development Department, Edinburgh.

Marcus, Christopher. 'Co-operative Hope for Housing' in *Building Design* (1982). February.

Matthews, Alison. *Management Co-operatives – The Early Stages* (1981). DoE, HMSO, London.

Molina, Humberto. 'Reactivacion Economica y Redistribuciondel Ingreso en la Politica de Vivienda' in *La Vivienda Popular Hoy en Colombia* (1981). Foro Nacional por Colombia, Bogota.

Molina, Humberto, et al. *Directorio Nacional de la Autoconstruccion* (1986). Servicio Nacional de Aprendizaje, Bogota.

Mondragon Luz Angela. 'Politica de Vivienda del Estado Colombiano' in *Colombia, Vivienda y Subdesarrollo Urbano* H. Molina (ed) (1979). CPU (Uninades)/FINISPRO, Bogota.

National Community Development Project Workers. *Whatever Happened to Council Housing?* (1976). Russell Press, Nottingham.

National Federation of Housing Associations. *Housing Associations: Their Contribution and Potential* (1984).

National Federation of Housing Co-operatives. *Secondary Co-ops Report* (1987).

National Federation of Housing Co-operatives. 'Argyll Street – A Shell Co-op' in *Around the Houses* No 8. 1984.

National Federation of Housing Co-operatives. 'Liverpool Labour Party Wrong About Co-ops' in *Around the Houses* August 1984

National Federation of Housing Co-operatives. Management Co-ops Group. *Tenant Management Co-ops – The Future* (1985).

Newell, Wendy. 'Scottish Co-ops De-privatised' in *Around the Houses* No 12. 1985.

Nicholson, Iain et al. *Community Ownership in Glasgow* (1985). Glasgow District Council, Glasgow.

Palacios, Marcos. *Coffee in Colombia 1850-1970* (1980). Cambridge University Press, Cambridge.

Payne, Geoffrey (ed). *Low Income Housing in the Developing World – The Role of Site and Services and Settlement Upgrading* (1984). John Wiley and Sons, Chichester.

Payne, Geoffrey. 'A Critique of the Gecekondus of Ankara' in *Self-Help Housing: A Critique* (1982). Alexandrine Press, Oxford.

Pickett, Kathleen. 'Merseyside's Population and Social Structure' in *Merseyside: Social and Economic Studies* Lawton and Cunningham (eds) (1970). Longman, London.

Reig, Martin. 'La Proyeccion de la Coexistencia de Formas de Produccion sobre la Morfologia Urban' in *Colombia, Vivienda y Subdesarrollo Urbano* (see above).

Rocha Sanchez, Lola. 'Ciudad Kennedy: A New Town in Bogota, Colombia' in *The Role of Housing in Promoting Social Integration* (1970). Department of Economic and Social Affairs, United Nations, New York.

Rosengard, Anne et al. 'Looking Backward – A Historical Perspective' in *Miles Better, Miles To Go – The Story of Glasgow's Housing Associations* (1985). The Housetalk Group, Glasgow.

Santana, Pedro, and Casasbuenas Constantino. *La Vivienda Popular Hoy en Colombia* (1981) Foro Nacional por Colombia, CINEP, Bogota.

Shearer, Janet. *Self-Help Community Housing Association* (1979). Unpublished dissertation, Department of Social Sciences, University of Bristol.

Skinner, R.J. et al. *People and Poverty – Problems of Self-Help Housing in the Third World* (1983). Methuen, London.

Smith, David. *Amenity and Urban Planning* (1974). Crosby Lockwood Staples, London.

Smith, Joan. *No Mean Fighter* (1974). Pluto Press, London.

Thompson, John. *Community Architecture: The Story of Lea View House* (1984). RIBA, London.

Thompson, Paul. *Socialists, Liberals and Labour – The Struggle for London 1885-1914* (1967). Routledge and Kegan Paul, London.

Topping, Phil, and Smith, George. *Government Against Poverty? Liverpool Community Development Project 1970-1975* (1977) Social Evaluation Unit, Oxford.

Toro, Eduardo et al. 'La Vivienda como Mercancia' in *Colombia, Vivienda y Subdesarrollo Urbano* (see above).

Torres, Camilo. 'Bogota, Pre-industrial City' in *Revolutionary Priest – The Complete Writings and Message of Camilo Torres* (1971) John Gerassi (ed). (1971). Jonathan Cape, London.

Treble, James H. *Urban Poverty in Britain 1830-1914*. Methuen, London.

Treble, James H. 'Liverpool Working-Class Housing 1801-1851' *The History of Working-Class Housing* S.D.Chapman (ed) (1971). David and Charles, London.

Turner, John. *Housing by People* (1982). 'Ideas in Progress' series, Open Forum, Marion Boyars, London.

Turner, John, and Fichter, R. *Freedom to Build* (1972). Collier Macmillan, New York.

Unidad Desarrollo Regional y Urbano. 'La Edificaion de Vivienda en Colombia' in *Revista de Planeacion y Desarrollo* (1982). Departamento Nacional de Planeacion. Bogota.

Vanegas, C.A. Velez. 'Accion Communal, Esfuerzo de Todos' and 'Integracion Progressiva' in *Revista de Autoconstruccion y Vivienda Popular* (1983 and 1984). Bogota.

Ward, Colin. *Tenants Take Over* (1974). Architectural Press, London.

Ward, Colin. *Housing: An Anarchist Approach* (1976) Freedom Press, London.

Ward, Colin. *When We Build Again* (1985). Pluto Press, London.

Wates, Nick. 'The Liverpool Breakthrough' in *Architects' Journal* 8 September 1982.

Westra, Jan. 'Lewisham Self-Build' in *Open House International* Vol 7(3) 1982. Eindhoven, Holland.

Whitman, David. 'The First 60 Years of Council Housing' in *The Future of Council Housing* (1982). Croom Helm, London.
Wohl, A.S. 'The Housing of the Working Classes in London 1815-1914' in *The History of Working-Class Housing* (see above).
Wright, Marian. *Possil Co-op Feasibility Study* (1984) Possil Housing Co-operative, Glasgow.